Sistah From Another Planet

BY DIANE VINCENT

Sistah from Another Planet

In the Name of the Most High
The Yielder, the Merciful

One of my favorite words is "indelible".
Usually I dedicate my books to my sons,
Shimon and James, and my mother Sadie
because they are the reason for which I write.
But there is a spirit that I want to celebrate
with this poetry book, because of the indelible
stain she has left in my life and the life of so many poets
This book is dedicated to you Giselle (Gi) Robinson
A beautiful indelible eternal spirit of poetry.

Table of Content

The Cosmo-Politician

"They ask me about my sexuality.
I told them I have no favorite color.
I love the earth, the moon, the sun
And all that is above below and in between --
It is in this same regard I show love."

Cream Sun Before the Father

Her petals thin and soft
When at first they bloomed baby pink hues,
Sweet with the nectar of innocence.
Her rose no longer a bud, yet indehiscent.
With the need to be nourished
She danced in the sun.
But what she consumed left her famished
Until she was visited by Sappho.

There in the cottage of her own emotions
She wept, realizing why she'd felt alone
All the while, adored by so many.

Enriched with a yen to free herself,
She submitted her inhibitions
And joined the feast prepared for she
And there she lay, in full bloom.
Shades of pink, now magenta
Like the creamy petals
Of the great willow herb.

Rosemary Savor

His love lingers like rosemary spices,
Perennial to my soul in the aftermath
Of the night before that invades my day
With memories of rose petals clinging to my libido episodes.
.

Castrating rosebuds,
She blossomed into full bloom erotica.

I am excited just by the thought of him
And his juices dripping like honeysuckle
Scented morning dew upon my lips, upon my legs.

Satisfied sessions in climatic climaxes,
Humidity higher than rapacious yearning,
His invasion explores the paries of me.
What I need is for him to implant
A reflection of we,
Like the lingering scents of rosemary spices--
Seasoning my sensuality that is compelled by the
Memoirs of an uninvited guest.
For the forbidden always taste the best.

Mayonnaise and Egg Sandwiches

I wanted to feel sex like she.
Her cravings were like hunger pains,
And like the lioness, she had to feed.

Mayonnaise and eggs sandwiches I would say,
Remembering how I adored watching my mother eat them,
Lips covered in the greasy cream I despised--
But was indoctrinated to love
Just by watching her.

Likewise my lover's sexual magnetism
Drew me in, taunted the pary
Of my very being.

I longed for her, not because I wanted her,
I wanted to be her.
Her pheromones emitting a soporific aphrodisiac
That lured her prey.

And as much contempt as I had for
Her dick fetish over me,
Her indiscretions, they excited me.
And like mayonnaise and egg sandwiches
I wanted to taste what she tasted,
I wanted to feel what she felt,
I wanted the insatiable craving
That possessed her to lewdness!
.

And each night as she mounted a different lover,
My heart would bleed with envy.

4

Yet I was ever the more aroused,
Climaxed by my vicarious affair
With she and her lovers
As if they had penetrated me.

The Jeweler

Her pearls lay upon her neck like a collection of jizm --
Erotic prisms reflecting the aftermath of pleasure.
Her gesture of elegance
Had me harder than wrought iron.

Do they not know it is the nobility
That is the most alluring?
It is the moniker you wish
To post your name upon.
It is holding the pillar and foundation
Of nations in the palm of your hand.
It is the precious stone, rare and priceless

She holds the divinity of my soul
In the canals of her merciful temple
That yields to the irrigation of man.

And I would replenish her land with
All the riches that my life can acquire
And lay them beneath her feet
So that she will know why I made the pearls.

The Soul of Summerland

And my lover dwells in the Summerland
Waiting for his ship to return
And bare him back to me.
For our souls bleed
Settling for no other.

I can only feel him in the apparitions
Of tainted realities
And painted images from death's sibling
Laughing and taunting me,
Imprisoning me in this parallel Sijiyn
Of densities and low vibrations,
Blocking his connection to me.

He sees me in Wiccan pastures--
In a material fetter of Hecate's Law.
His fervent love longs to rescue my sorrow—lamenting
For he cannot kiss away my tears,
He cannot caress away my fears.
Yet our spirits are linked.

And in the hollowness of my heart,
Whereupon my bed I lay
I hear his mantra desperately chanting
"Let faith guide you...
Let love guide you."

Lipcolade

He touches my lips with the tips of his passion.
Tracing my face it abrades my defenses,
Polishing my soul like fine stones.
Brushing his fingers across my face,
I feel the king has granted me grace
To dwell in his kingdom of compassion.

Like the moth drawn to light my body
Yields submitting to his friendly invasion,
Bringing me gifts of drunken libation
And blanketing me with days of he and I
Gone by in futures passing.

He orbits around my atoms and
Caresses my nucleus. Electrons
Send impulses that communicate with
My Constant Elation where a sun
Called 'Mm' is born.

We are linked, as he takes a jaunt
Down the prickly sensation to the
Carnal cord of my belly's eye.
The ocean of abyss is at high tide
When he sets sail upon the shores
Waxed away of its bristly sands
Awakening currents that bevel
Like fresh hanging sheets exposed
to torrent winds whispering Aahh,

Sticky sweet incursion betrays my
Private fortress, taking me captive.
I'm imprisoned by ecstasy
Heralding in tongue and member.

He touches me with the tips of his
Passion that will eternally haunt
My conscious like poignant ashes,
Memoirs of an inferno consuming
The innocence of a jeweled temple.

Where is Love

She speaks like the shyness
And quiet sun shower
Upon sweet flowers,
Scenting them with her love.
She has not the power
Of roar and thunder --
Lightening tearing asunder
Old roots.
Scorching fate dries her words like raisins.
This humble fruit... sweet,
Grazing meadows with a brazen appeal
Trying to be heard.
Her attempt foiled by the zenith sun.
Her sweet dew dissipates and becomes
Vapors to return a quiet sun shower,
In the hour of Asr,
Desperately searching for that faithful one.

The Dance of the Infidel

My fall from grace unregretful,
Beckoned by the calls from the flashes of yellow,
Red, purple, and green against the blackest velvet.
Disrobing my innocence kept in covert sanctuaries of iniquity.
There is no Pentateuch here to blame me, no sin to bind me.

Circumcise this skin of inhibition and mutilate my diffidence.
I want to dance the flatterer's dance and become a pillar of salt.
For I look back on the righteousness I spent in the arms of the
infidel --
And I watched love rush in and out, passing through my youth,
While I nourished myself on sweet gall.

Bathe me with kisses upon the open altar
And caress my shameless nudity.
For I am purified from your repugnant morality,
And find my freedom on Debauchery's Road."

Red Rains April's Pain

She saved me with the soul of Baha'ism.
Turned the downtrodden into a man.
Washed my filth with the hem of her dress
And purified my viced blood with her hymns

'Twas the nagging of my timorous soul that turned blessings to gall,
As red rains April's pain, dripping from these cowardly hands.
For she would have me no more.

And as my tears washed away the blood stained knife
I knelt above her watching as my world drained from her veins.

And I wept not because the orb of my life lay beneath me.
Because of the shameful cravenness that provoked me
To take her life and spare mine own.
For I could not bear to know that she could live without me.

The Carrier

Hurts like hell this six plus hour tread of catch-up.
Each ache and pain, punishment for my lack of
Discipline, fortitude and determination.
Yet I wage on, loads heavy upon my back --
Scratching at gravel in quicksand
Trying to pull me back down into its disenfranchise abyss.
Yet the paddle of my feet beating pavement
Pulls me to the surface,
Just enough to see the end of my journey.
So I wage through this muck, and mundane --
For I know Kawthar is within my reach.
And how I love the taste of hemp milk and honey.

I Am The Fool Who Falls

He feeds me complexities
With his worrisome eyes,
And I wonder what pains him inside.
Until the day comes when I give him some,
And now he looks like he's just fine.
And I am the fool who falls. ☹

Coloreds

Brownstones, Boogie down Bronx,
Harlem and BK Brooklyn.
I see beautiful colors
Dancing outside my window,
Moving in rhythms from rapid vibrations
Elevating to majestic potentials.

Colors flowing to the ritual drum
Beats reminiscent of the barrios in Cuba,
Or the Caribbean, dancing to the rhythm of
The babalao, casting the spells of Obeah.

Earthly hues stained with soil
Torn by the weather of time,
Infected like the blankets of
Paisley, covering indigenous blood--
Building cities, laying railroads
Creating beats and tones, crossing
Boundaries, climbing plateaus.

Phenomenal colors outside my window--
Mahogany, cedar, oak, vines intertwine
With olive and pine, rich as the
Blackberry and concord grapes running
Rich from root to stem-- stretching their
Limbs across the world like lightening
Strikes the heavens with might and power.

These colors emit the world, smiling in bevels,
Raising above the abraded earth with a bow
And a promise that colors shall never drown
Again, but will be blanketed by rivers
Of blazing reds and smokeless
Fire for ignoring the sun.

Drink She Wine Pon De Night

Come dance wit me pon de twilight
where de city lights gleam
Like rivers and streams of gold and coal
And cars beat pon de man hole covers
Like a percussionist on steel pan drums.
Sway ye hips Ma.

Drink she wine pon de night.
Dutty wine pon me wild.
Be I beguild.
Skin smooth like de flow of
Melted caramel.

Tenacious is ya sex appeal
Almost as surreal and enticing
As a wet dream.
Dance wit me Mommy
Down to ya river
Of milky tears of joy
And bathe in yellow, green, orange,
Blue, red and purple delight.
Come dance wit me pon de twilight

Let me vibrate pon ya cotton candy
And shake ya shimmy Ma
Fair pon de eyes ya blow me mind
Come dance wit me pon de twilight
Move she hips all around
Drink she wine pon de night
Dutty wine pon me wild
Dutty wine pon me right
Beautiful lady
Come dance wit me pon de twilight.

Titled Unspoken

I have always been afraid to tread deep waters.
But I would die a thousand times if I could
Submerge myself in an ocean of climatic libations.

Sticky things I quickly wash away.
Yet your aftermath I long to lay and relish
Just long enough to remember how it feels.

I usually avoid salt at all cost.
Yet the salty taste of you, I would consume
Time and time again letting it savor in my soul.

From illness and battery I abscond.
Yet to be afflicted with the fever and convulsions
From your powerful strokes I would eagerly
Enslave myself.

In anger I have never raised my voice.
Yet somehow in a rage of passion and frenzy
I scream out your name.

I have never been provoked to belligerence.
Like a crazed beast I groan grunt and
claw your flesh with each stroke that
spots my G, causing my body to hemorrhage
with the constant flows of milk and cream.

I have always been warned about eating
After someone.

Still the thought of your tongue invading
my mouth I hunger for,
To taste my juices upon your lips.

I have always had my limits and boundaries.
Now the threshold to my desires are free,
Uninhibited and unlimited.
I will travel with you from the blessed
Land of milk and honey to Sodom
And rest in your erotic temple
Governed only by the aphorisms of
Your lovemaking.

Equinox

The equinox lies in the birth of the Nubian,
The acceptance from the Negro,
The transformation of the colored,
The revelation of the African American,
And the assassination of the Nigga

In the Field of Lilies

My soul was complete in my temple
Until arrogance evaded it with corruption
Teaching fearlessness, yet living in such a
Trepidation, words shackled the truth
And imprisoned my potential.

Castrating fond memories
My spiritual growth temporarily fettered--
My devotion abashed by lies
Replaced with pain and betrayal.

I feel like I'm on a kaleidoscope ride
Trying to find the right path leading
To my completion.
And I rise and fall, rise and fall
Ascend and descend in spirit,
Knowing all that I was exposed was not all a lie
For I have seen the sun rise on many of these truths.
Yet I refuse to take hold of roses with thorn stems
When I can just as easily plant my own from
Someone willing to provide the seeds
That sow spirituality -- potential, strength and righteousness
So that I may reap the fruits that will nourish my soul
And transform me into the goddess I deserve to be.

I am an open, precious vessel, tarnished from usury,
Ready to be polished with unshakable faith, sincerity
Truth, love, wisdom and strength.
But-- I have lost trust in mortals

So I pray the Most High will send me a gardener,
And the vision to discern his/her holistic, organic veracity.

Whose words will flow with truth like the rivers of Kawthur,
Whose motives will be as pure as the silk from a spider
And nourishing as the sap that feeds the tree of heaven.
For the season of reaping is at hand
and I stand in the mist of Lilies hoping
to be picked.

My Space

Thank you for sharing your space,
A space stamped in time,
As memoirs of the birth of love --
Energy that cannot be extinguish in the universe.
For it, along with hate, are all
Part of the continuity in this
Conundrum we call life.
Thus love is as you are,
Stamped forever in my space

In All Honesty

I conceived my shame before I grew hair on my private
When I pleaded with Maria not to tell my sister that David and I
had compared genitals in the stairway hole behind the building.
Later voices with higher learning would determine the act to be
natural for someone Of five suns.
However, the leather that tore into my flesh bellowed
resonances of shame and fornications.

I conceived my shame before I grew hair on my private
When my brother knocked on my bedroom door to beckon me to
watch.
The circus light shined dim on mommy and daddy.
Its light would be the lighthouse to my passion in years to come.

I conceived my shame before I grew hair on my private.
French kissing Eric grinding in the janitor's closet.
The stench of the mildew mop burned my nose
But did not encumber the hump and grind.

I conceived my shame before I grew hair on my private.
As I came back to David who would kiss and fondle my bare A
cups,
His breath smelling like the stale scent of crabs and cigars that
waft throughout his apartment.

I conceived my shame about the time I grew hair on my private
And fell in puppy lust with Gregory Hill, just thirteen suns as he
'faced' me in the cold, dank, cemented Broadway movie theater.
His tongue stroking my clit (facing), my mind wondering how in
the hell did he know how to do it.

I gave birth to my shame when I took no value in my precious jewels.
Allowing a man I love not, to part the oyster and steal my pearl.

I gave birth to my shame when I took another's innocence knowing I would probably never settle for Kirk. The biggest shame having shooed away the only man I came close to any emotions that would simulate love.
He is my best friend, will be 'till my end.

I gave birth to my shame when I used eyes as a factor to birth my child,
Conceived in the back of a bookstore, climaxing without love.
Like a harlot I laid saying, "If prostitutes can, so can I."

I gave birth to my shame when I realized I'd never had sex with someone I truly loved or was even physically attracted.

I gave birth to my shame when she kissed me and exposed a latent side of me...to me.

I gave birth to my shame when I sacrificed all that is right to love all that is wrong,
Knowing the love I had could never and would never be reciprocated.

I laid down my shame by the sea of hurt and realization that I must first learn to love me before I can allow anyone else into my heart.

.

I Blame Mother

Killing curiosity I would sneak in
Their room at night.
I saw how sensual she was,
How much she was into her love making--
The satisfaction on her face, in her tone.

So I asked allured by the thought of her,
"What turned you on about Daddy?"
"He eats pussy good."
Just like that she said.
She was always open like that.

Oh how I loved it.
I wanted to feel that sensuality.
I wanted sex to satisfy me that way.

She said, "Your first experience is going to be so good."
I bled pain. Not good.

It is because of her words I am still looking.
For I remain unappeased.
It is because of her words I do not prejudice my search.

Had she not said those words
would I have been content with what I've received?

I blame my mother
Ole Scorpion

22 Lewis Avenue

Its clouded hues are illusions
In my repose
Dark and dim with
Visions branded on my conscious
And subconscious of broken elevators
Going to basement floors that don't exist,
Corridors to halls where the pungent stench
Of the janitor's mop seeped out closets.
And I rise and fall in the broken elevator
Sometimes crashing to a basement floor that
Didn't exist.

Sometimes I'd rise beyond the seventh floor where
My memories tore into my nights of
My mother's return from the grave in
The only state I regretfully remember her,
Enslaved by Old English fighting to seek refuge
In the streets of Bed-Stuy.
And I lose her for days at a time.
Shamed by my memories, I
Gaze seven stories down
Wondering if I could survive the jump.
Would I reach the tree to break my fall?
The leap, a jump off the barrels or
Monkey bars of Pity Pat Park.
Sometimes it proved to be deadly.

Sometimes I would jump escaping the vampires
And I would fly traversing the skies and discovering
New worlds towards Bushwick lands and beyond
"I can fly" I would say, although sometimes I'd
Barely escape the ground.
My father always the same...

Old -- trying to survive his diabetes,
although he didn't actually develop
it until he was way beyond the walls of 7E.
And finally I would awake ashamed I did
my mother no justice in my memory of her.

22 Lewis, still remembering the stench of the janitor's closet:
where I and Eric at eight, French kissed and grinded, the
only male I loved (at the time),
where I and David played Helen Keller in the back
of the front stairwell, whichever was the emptiest at the time
or smelt less of piss than the other. Probably the only male I
ever loved (at the time).
where I and Gregory Hills kissed. He asked me if
I loved him, and I told him yes, because I knew
that's what he wanted to hear -- although he just might have
been the only male I ever really loved or came close to it (at the
time)

It's been years since I've drank a shot of arduous memories of
the alcohol abuse, the drunken seizures in front of our stoop,
playing doctor, making sure the belt or spoon kept
Manny from swallowing his tongue,
watching Smokey trip so low on his synthetic high,
we were sure he'd hit the grown.

Death of a friend in that broken elevator
that went to basements that didn't exist
as he futilely escapes a predator, crushed by
the broken elevator going beyond the seven floors

I fight back tears and sip on fond
thoughts from Johnny pumps, Bushwick pools and Poppie
carrying me all the way home because someone stole my brand
new

lime green Pro Keds. Loved him for that... still

Pity Pat Park, tray bags and Old English, jacks
and Johnny Ho, Hot Peas and Butter, Run Catch and Kiss
Relay Racing, Skelly, metal skates with the keys to tighten them,
homemade skate boxes, Double Dutch, Hop Scotch
basketball, baseball, football, block parties,
fireworks and that you show me yours and I show you mine dare
that got my ass tore up. (angry face at Maria for telling), bodega
hoagies, Chinese flix at the Broadway rat infested movie
theatre.
Crunching up together in the dank cold cement building,
relishing and memorizing every Bruce Lee and Lady Kung Fu
kck and punch.

And although my repose may be invaded by dim apartments,
unjust memories of Sadie, everyone's trip and excursion, ice
cream cone and cookies mama -- and broken elevators that went
to basements that didn't exist, I will always treasure my 22
Lewis peeps.

Silhouette of a Perfect Phase

She laid there bare, as if he'd molded her that way,
Watching how the moon copied silhouettes from his godly frame.
The sinews of his chest that were just moments ago arched in
The curves of her back, as he whispered how good she felt,
Were dancing with each breath he took, commanding her own
To move in sync with his.

And for a moment she feared losing him,
In dread of losing her own breath or the beat of her heart.
She rose from the bed letting her left foot sweep away the
residual design
Their bodies symmetrically made upon the pearl silk satin sheets.

Inhaling she held it until he was locked within her arms,
Her nipples cooled by the chill of his back from the evening
breeze.
Pressing herself close she exhaled
And mentally merged her molecules with his --
The heat off her breath sending her electrons to meet his,
Creating an electrical impulse from their friction.
For even their chemistry could not keep from binding them as
one.

Stroking his neck with the swelling of her lips,
Her hands wandered to the mound of his chest finding his
erogenous zone.
His breathing became heavy as his body melted to her touch --
All but his passion, which throbbed like a sky full of cumulus
clouds
Spewing streaks of lightening across its density.

A spark of life was birthed from the vibrating waves
Traveling adverse the kundalini into the carnal abode of Nun,
Where she yielded her mercy and cradled it,
Incubating a love so strong its molecules quickly began to
multiply.

She laid there with him still inside closing her walls around him
Until she could feel the heaviness become deeper and deeper
And the weight of his might was too much to bear.
Gently she rolled him over and rested in the remnants of him.
Facing him, she inhaled the traces of her flower in full bloom.

Kind Heart

Trapped in an abyss like a diamond in coal,
You've washed the soot off my heart and soul,
So that a precious jewel shines forth.
It's priceless --
And I willingly give it to you.
Thank You Luv

Earthly

My hands have traveled this earth
In different countries.
My feet rest upon its soil.

They say your earth is your soul.
I believe that now.
For in this part of earth I now reside
It welcomes me with nutrients
I've never consumed before.

My hands caress its firm brown soil
Dyed with a rich redness,
Like chocolate when I eat it.
And oh how I loved to eat and breathe it.

Its musky, chalky scent
Revitalizes a sensation and craving in me.
And the more I inhale
The more it stimulates me
To do whatever I can to make
This earth a better place to reside.

So as I lay upon the soil
I stroke its grass
Sometimes braiding it.
Its rocks are rich with minerals
Erotically formed like the
Temple of Khajuraho,
Enticing me to stroke it,
Guiding my fingers over each sensual curve
Visiting each crevice and cavern.

How beautiful is the temple of this earth.

And I often visit inside just to praise it
With oral accolades,
Wandering through its trimmed bushes
And lovely fragrant flowers in full bloom,
Sweet like honeydew melon.
This earth has become the soul of me.
Therefore it is where I wish to reside
And nourish myself for an earthly eternity.

Tell Me What It Smells Like

She marked her territory
With juices brewed from the
Loin of Lillith and Hatshetsup,
Formed the flesh of Aphrodite,
And tasted like mandrake delights,
Sprinkled upon the altar in the
Temples of Khajuraho
Burning smokeless fires of desire.

For sixty nine moons
It scents the root vortex of my bride.
Three centuries and six decades
Sweet milky tears of joy
Flow from her nectar,
Marking her territory,
So that all will know
The spoor of her love
Is indelible and affianced.

And when Atum falls,
The sweet willow herb
Is in full bloom

She is SoulReal

Her smile reveals warmth and solace,
Yet cannot umbrella the pain and struggle in her eyes.
She is strong, focused and a conqueror of deadly obstacles.
So she knows this challenge, she will also prevail.
To market this strength, melt it down and bottle it could
Change so much of the world.

The depth of her dimples lead a pathway to where
I would willfully journey,
A soulful place -- joyful place;
A land with a sky filled with
A spectrum of intellect and perfection.

Her sol shines bright within her world.
And I bathe in its essence, purifying myself
Just before I dare request to enter her temple,
Where I receive the communion
Of Goddesses Bast and Hathor,
In a land built before Sappho,
Where passionate, erotic and exotic fruits are served
With milk and honey drinks
Flavored with amaretto and cinnamon,
And served by Aphrodite.

Rivers of lime flow fluent currents
And climax upon shores that lay bare to the world.
I am nourished abundantly and haunted
With an insatiable avarice that will undoubtedly
Keep me coming back to be appeased.

Kham Nehisi

Locs dress his crown,
Majestic black Nubian,
God of mother earth.

His spirit, pure
Awakens the conscious mind,
Manifests self- love.

Cowry shell necklace,
Red, yellow and green --
Stellar God, I am your Earth.
Lay upon my lap
Let me stroke away pain.

Beautiful Brown Skin,
This is but my accolade
To thank you for being a --
Majestic... Black... Nubian...

Untitled Passion

As smooth as caramel
She drips her beauty onto pages.
And viewing her tastes oh so sweet.
It feels just right admiring her,
In spite of what others may think.

I travel the lines that encompasses her lips,
Like pathways into jaunts of pleasure,
Thinking of ways to enjoy them,
Circumventing her inhibited sutra.

She leans into her interest as if
She is luring her lover to play.
Her responses are like soft caresses,
That satisfy her lover.

He cares for her.
For he knows it's his words
That moves her deep within.

And I can only live in the
Tormented realm of vicariism.
For if she were tangible to me,
We could soar the skies above the Delhi
Into Khajuraho and furlong within the temple,
Where I would bathe her with amaretto kisses,
Feast upon her lotus like feasting on mandrake delights,
In her reservoir of sweet milky tears of joy.

And each time she revisits the domain
I will beseech her in my heart
To soar with me to those erotic grounds,
Where we shall share aphrodisiac pleasures
For 69 moons.

Holes in my Ho-ism

Tears in a bowl
Tired and broken
Didn't make me stronger
Poor man's song

He said that's why I didn't have shit
Talkin' about my pussy
And unwillingness to freely give it

And sometimes
sitting on a black folding stress
I wish it was in me

Ho be it
They got a hustle
Smart ones anyway
Money on their mind
But ain't a problem in
Their pockets

What don't break ya
Fear, Fibroids, Fag
Got holes in my Ho-ism
At lease by their ideas
Maybe it's true
That's all it takes

Nevertheless bills due
Right about now
Sad though

Tears in a bowl
Tired and broken
Didn't make me stronger
Same ole song.

Bullshit Intellectuals

Quick to regurgitate the wisdom
From others who deemed themselves godly
Enough to tell someone else what's what.
Wanting to be respected for their ideologies.

And I see them as foolish as the street magicians --
Who, in my respect, fakes potential with foolish feats.
They are illusionist.
For if their intellects were to be so praised,
Honored and respected,
There would be no wars,
There would be a cure for the hungry,
Diseased and afflicted.

So as far as I'm concerned,
Your rhetorical secretion
Is just redundant prattle --
A scourge that smites the life in the party.
Kiss my ass.

3C=K

I do not speak of faces burned from
Chemicals and environmental circumstance
For I absconded that life in the bearing of witness
Faces tarnished, tightened, contorted
Set in eyes, skin on bone, fat consumed
By ether.

I do not speak of cosmetic artist
With harlot convictions
Painting layers of ignorance
Immolating beasts
Whipped by mothers with hide
That have no roots, culture,
Consciousness, self-love.
For they'd get better results
Flagging a beast of burden with
A cattle prod to coerce him
to carry them into
the surreal realm behind pearly gates

I cannot feel the spirit
From inspirational gibber
Holy scat confounding
Souls sold by the mimics
Of Colonial incantations.

What were you before the invocation?
Auction, gibbet, flags and scars
Exposing raw shame, emasculation and blame
Black coal crumbled and tarred

Lost your land culture and gods
Ancestors cry out to the Insaan (Man, the forgetful)
Light black kneel before anorexic ghost
With forsaken allegiance
For the gas of oppression
High from fabrications seeking salvation
And your ancestors wait in
Awareness to lift you back
To your throne
In the ocean of truth
'Tis where you'll sail
To the King's home
Fire, earth, wind, and water
Upon the altar of Neter (Nature)
Regurgitate his spiritual disease

Brainwash this pale wilderness
And command the earth, filament
Cosmos
Oh 9 ether spirit of Al Kuwn (the universe)
Get from beneath his umbrella
For there is no reign upon your head

May your kingly crown be unpressed and fried.
Come out from behind the lies
And lay in the salvation of
Culture, Consciousness, Community.

In Kinship cometh thy Kingdom

I Smile

A blush from an initial thought
Comforts like the waves of the sun,
Caressing my body with warmth,
Tormented by the winter solstice.

The gentle breeze that brushes
The ocean's shores, like the security
Of a mother's gentle stroke upon
Her infant's brow.
You invoke a tender smile
Of reverence and admiration.

When I'm with you, it's a place
Where only lovers go --
A place of heaven and happiness --
A place of peace and contentment.

My need for you is essential, pure and insatiable.
You're my breath of life on which I depend.
Crippling is the thought of losing you.

Shall a fetus develop outside the mercy
Of its mother's womb?
Shall the hummingbird not sing?
Joining the bee, he spreads life and love.
So, how shall I live without you?

Your love is the plasma to my soul,
Sweet as honey dew
The nectar that nourishes my desires.

This craving is tenacious.

Coal covered diamond,
A jewel that transformed this
Poor wretched form
Into a pure, rich soul,
Whose spirit reflects the joy of your presence.

You are a blue light, waves of intellect,
Inspirational and pure, unconditional love --
The scent of wilderness, images of colorful
Terrain and discovery of new life
Upon ocean floors.

A kiss from you is savory like the salt
That washes upon the banks of the Nile.
I breathe in you and exhale freedom.
I smile.

Abyss

The light peers out from the darkness.
Trapped -- Abyss' are not good,
When scented with fettered indoctrinations,
Inhaling noxious bullshit and
Exhaling fear, doubt, and excuses --
Clawing at your existence,
Mauling potential.

Light becomes too far to fetch.
And a wretched soul is a wretched soul,
Wasting in the darkness trapped.
And abyss' are never good
But to survive sometimes you have
To shut out the unattainable light,
Until you find that strength to fight
Through the darkness or --
Find balance.

At Last I'm In Love

You define me like no other.
You've fulfilled me like a flowing stream
in a sea of continuity.

I need not touch the sun to be nourished
by its rays.
In this way I am rewarded by the glory
of existence from the beauty of words --
vibrating on tones that nourish my soul.

Silent resonance echo in the acoustic
Dimensions of black and white.
I need not search any longer for love
For I am here.

I am indeed in love --
With a tenacious yearning --
Insatiable yet complete.
For without it I am void --
An empty mass of redundancy,
plagued with a plaque of mundane.

This challis from which I drink
Is crafted with divine materials,
Composed of spiritual essence.

I love you Word. And they have named
you today,   Poetry.

The Extinction

There are many Nubian poets
But our appreciation for them has died
Thus there will be no more rise
Of the infamous vestige of
"Negro" "Black"
"African American" poets
The Chronicles of the 21st Century
Has closed their pages
And last prophet has fallen
In the complacency of intergration.

Although the sun of word still rises
And creativity reigns abound
Raining black ink upon pages
Creating an incandescence
That forms colorful spectrums
From beautiful verses
Emitting the mouth of poets, the pens of poets
Second to second, minute to minute
Hour to hour
Each one interwoven and
Elapsing the other.

You cannot shut us out
The graves, tomes
And mausoleums were not
Meant to bury the future
But to give birth to a continuity
Of Nubian poets and activists
Appreciated and known by our

Future generations
Sprouting each season
Lasting like the evergreen.

We are here and will not be
Syncopated by the weakness
Of sellouts, sycophants and conformity
Scourged and suppressed
By protocols and plots
We are not your profit dollar

We are revolution of consciousness
And revelation of social change
And we will break through your
Cloud of smoke and mirrors
To shine like the sun
To pour down like the rain
To flood like the waters
The future nation of New Beings (Nubian)
Our presence, our worth, our time
Our relevance, our necessity
The poet is here
And we will be documented

Unfaithful

We form deceptions with false promises
We know not for sure we will keep.
Riding on wings of white lies
We believe fate would grant us truths.

But in the hidden abyss of circumstances
And the musky scent of magnetism and pheromones
I lay another upon my bed,
Slaying truths with pleasure and passion,
Repenting in the sticky aftermath.

This nature is strong in me
Like the need for the lioness to hunt.
Heedless of gender she consumes the
Nectars of her prey.

Although I relish in your
Den the companionship,
It is my nature to feed.
This desire was spliced into my gene
By my progenitors.

And as you bear witness to my
Broken pledge from scuttlebutt,

Know that I love you and only you truly,
Yet the latency of lust
Will indubitably subjugate my love.
And I look upon you shamed with contrition,
Realizing that I have finally lost you.

Wasteland

All of your empty promises have
Been shuttled in and out of my life
With your lies and inconsistencies.
And now I am like a wasteland,
Dry of any emotions for you,
And contaminated by the bullshit you
Left behind.

Now I have to dowse myself
With the fragrance of affairs
Just to rid myself of the poignant stench
Of each memory of you.

For if I do not, then I will
See the world as ugly as you
Have left my heart.

The Music Of Suhaila

I thought discovering you was a gift.
But now I sift through the images
And places where my mind drifts
When you play into my ear, and --
You make me feel alone.

Enslaved by your tones resonating
In my soul, and I yearn to have her near.

If I had a clue --
I would have never unwrapped you --
Releasing you to tap into my latent secrets --
Feelings that I was comfortable with
Keeping inside, now vulnerable.
You've opened wide a portal plagued
With regret.

I pray time and time again,
But some words never reach that
Immortal end.
Maybe I need to depend on my
Own wings must I take flight.

Imprisoned by complexities
I don't know how I'll rest at ease.
I remain unappeased
Seeing her only when I close my eyes
At night.

With a tenacious craving my body cries,
Substitute with lies and illusions
I can only dream of touching her,

Kissing her in that ethereal place.

When I opened you, you opened me so wide,
No longer hide, I'm set bare
My secrets inside,
A gibbet upon my face.

When you look at me, really what you see,
Is the reality of your mind's eye,
Images as real as anything tangible.
Therewith I structure my state,
Recreate that beautiful
And burn it on my mental plate --
A desperate attempt to employ the physical.

What the fuck is this?
What path did I dismiss
To detour in this abyss?
Tormented by loneliness and void,
I'm drowning in it.

This redundant session of depression.
Fuck this confession.
Staring down a steel barrel
I wish I had the courage to put an end
To this shit.

It's amazing what the power of tone can do.
But I don't blame you.
Got to admit it's true.
You have a gift more effective
Than you probably even know.
Peace my sistah, keep the flow.

Redundancy

Friends melt away like wax.
Remnants of my past and future elapse
staining the plates of my psyche --
once illuminating my life and calming my soul.

Yet I can only offer them my back.
For I am like the achene of a dandelion.
"Take charge of your own destiny", they say.
I want to possess my fate
No more than I welcome the
Loneliness and pain that accompanies it.

The wind inevitably carries me against my will
Leaving the seeds to sow sorrow
and haunts my neglected heart.

Shackled Stallion

I caressed his smooth
glowing black frame.
My hands gently gliding
across his locs.
His legs strong -- powerful.
His chest broad and proud.
His head stout -- held high.

I would dream of the days
and nights I would mount him
as bare as a fresh yearling.
I would ride him into an endless
pasture of freedom and joy
enraptured in his black majesty.

When I was away I longed to return
To his side -- fresh, wild with ambition.
Willing to challenge any obstacle,
Jumping hurdles and leaping
enormous bounds.

Then like a beat he was bound.
Chained like stone.
Blood fire raced through his temples.
They could not fetter his mind.
though behind gray eyes his spirit is torn,
his potential maimed.

Yet in the hollow abyss of his defeat
He remains an exponent

Of the strength of our ancestors --
Their spirits, like the fresh scent of dew.
And I saw freedom come.

And in the hour of 'Asr
He would tread upon the joyful blades
crying out in the wind --
Ankh Hotep! Ankh Hotep!
That is to say --
Everlasting Peace! Everlasting Peace!

The Offering

Mantle me with brown silk
And heat me with salty oils scented from lust.
Ignite my passion with dirty vapors,
Until this caldron swelters and combusts.

Cool my insatiety with the ashes
From my singed iridescent flower,
Filled with the sap of your tree of life
'Til I belch my appeasement,
And rekindle the flame
That illuminates my incandescent shrine,
And the offering of nectar is devoured.

Umberluv

My umber love, I worship your frame.
Nile ruler, soul of my plane, god is your name.
But do you remember how great you are?
Do you see the traces of your scar?
Blinded to self and kind, you Nod, wandering far.

Forsaking your own melanin,
You surrender your integrity within.
Remember and reprise?
Echoes of your past in the garden,
Moods in your eyes.
Reminiscent of your glory
You were taught to despise.
Bestowing a gift, your seed is a prize.
The source of every race.

Prime throughout time,
The Most High has given you His grace.
Yet you disgrace, embrace and
Taste every face outside your place.
Come back to my love.
Graze in the pastures of my strawberry fields.
Let me honour your Supreme Being
And bring forth your fruit my mercy yields.

Master of molecules,
You've reversed your density.
From nine to six, six to nine,
You've consumed false chemistry.
The vines are intertwined

And you're out of your mind.
My umber love, I worship your frame,
Yourself and your kind.
My umber love I worship your frame.
Nile ruler, soul of my plane,
God is your name.

Armor Up

It is the shield against ignorance.
It can smite illiteracy,
Pierce poverty,
Set ablaze stigmas and stereotypes,
Wage war on prejudice,
Nukes trendy soldiers,

Usurped misinformation,
Unshackles chains and melts bars,
Feed the hungry,
Cure the mundane,
And restore nations.

It is the enemy to obtuseness.
It is the needle pushing itself
Through the thick fibers of life,
Trying to thread together
The history of the Negro's struggle to achieve,
And the Nigga's rebellion to forget.
It is Education.
Armor up and fight in the techno illogical war
To eradicate Education

Oh Woman Thou Art Loved

I wanted to show you love,
Definitive and intimate as honey
Is to a bee.

I wish I could nourish you
With love like the rays of Ra
That sustains the life of a flower,
So that you would blossom with
The beauty it has given you
To show the world.

Clouds mantle not the beauty of the world.
Its gray hue is not the beast
That beats upon happiness.
It rains down a personification of purification,
Purging the world of filth,
So that when the sun does shine,
Beauty can be restored -- in time.

Likewise, pain and suffering are purgatories
That exists in many hues.
And our tears cleanse the wounds
Of the heart so that the rays of love
Will shine and the beauty of the world
Can once again blossom in the life of the
Afflicted.

You deserve to be loved, all of you --
Held in the arms of a lover,
Caressing your brow,

Lips kissing away the pain
In each tear that falls,
Massaging the stress away
That hides within your being.

Loves cries out like a child in peek-a-boo play.
Its taunting cries call out repeatedly
"You can't find me, you can't find me."
But at last my gentle touch lures it out --
And it greets me transformed into your smile.

You deserve nothing more
Than to be cloaked with love
And let the strength of passionate arms
Embrace and mantle you from
The fear that depletes your divinity.

If I could show you all love definitive and intimate...
And if you remember anything of me --
Remember this.
For this is what you deserve.

Snapped

She takes a sip contemplating the consequences.
But the open hands and balled fist she can't endure alone.
The strong ether, pungent and bitter, slides down warm,
Caressing her pain and nulls her weak disposition.

She is a vessel for the spirits to embody her.
She knows they will take up residence and would
Be almost impossible to evict.

But they in all their malevolence (male violence)
Like the cherubs that guard the gates of Eden
Will protect her, be her brave warriors
With the delight to battle.
And she will gain the strength to protect the afflicted.

She takes another sip of this poignant toxin
Conjuring up the jinn from gin mills
Possessing her as did her progenitors.
She knows she's reached the point
She cannot return on her own.

All the pain trapped inside is stimulated by the ether
And vibrates rapidly like hydrogen into helium
And helium into hydrogen,
Transforming pain into anger.

She explodes with ruthless blows.
Her blade tears into him time and time again.
Blood fills fleshy black holes
And a Marid has been born --
A Manito that is evil and callous in every form.

The oppressor, now weakened, is gone
But the demon inside her lives on.
Will the love for her children be her exorcist?
Will it be enough for her to quit
As she makes the choice to heal or be healed?

Under the Umbrella I See a Rainbow

Her finger tips stretch softly across his strong jawline.
He looks into the windows of her soul and sees himself there.
Loving her is essential. Needing his love is involuntary.

The grass supports her and her partner like a magic carpet ride.
This scenic route through life has sent them on a journey of love.
Her full lips kiss her on her neck, melting away
The crust of despise and judgmental contempt.

And I gaze upon it all, standing there in the park.
I am so in love with love.
It is the shade for hate, loneliness and void
And I vicariously share their love as if I was the center and
they encompass me.

Aware of love's ability to also harm with intense acrimony.

And thus, I enjoy visiting it much like the presence and beauty
of a baby that is not mine own.
For I can always give it back before it shits on me

The Venerable Caterpillar

My ascending cries
Become raised assumptions,
Washed away in futileness.
For I am smitten by a
Handicap change
And the one to receive
My ocean of love manifests not.

Thus I am left to drown in
My own secretion.
Passion building so, it smothers
Each gentle touch I yearn to give.

Caressing massages are shackled
By the malignancy of solitude.
Yet my mind torments my lips
With the feel of an apparition
In my morning dreams.

And I fiend vicariously in
The witness' pew,
Famished by my own
Trepidation,
Scorned by my own realizations.
And those who've mastered
Their fears feast at the
Table of love.

Alas, if I could just catch
But a crumb from their plate,
I could taste my lover upon my tongue.

Desperate I settle for the manna

Reserved for the ones with low esteem,
With just enough nectar to know that
I still pump these feeling through my veins.

Mine eyes affixed wide by my desires
And delight in the aesthetic faculties
Of love shared in the world
Of the left handed by she two.

No one can understand
Why my silence is louder
Than my cries.

The Window Jumper

Tis my final destination,
for I do not have the strength
to find my purpose in life.
Therefore there will be no
manifestation no fruition,
and it was better that I had
not been born.

And a Negro with lost hope
Is better a Negro that is no more.
Tis my final destination -- destiny nation...
The place my soul will dwell.
And I take this leap every day when I feel
Like I'm losing hope.

Thank God I'm too much of a coward
And to addicted to this beautiful sadist
Called life.

In the Realm of Jacob's Ladder

I lost the jewel of faith
That comfort of certainty
Smitten by self-indulgence and corruption
Replace with unsettling reality
Colder than the Alaskan skies
In the winter solstice
Darker than the deepest part of Nun

Now there is no deciphering
The spiritual, esoteric, supernatural
From the powers of the mind
And that which is real

In this realm of Jacob's ladder
Perhaps I've just become functionally mad
At any rate, there is no resolve
Futilely fretting the inevitable
And the unknown.

A Black Woman's Lamentation

I lay upon my earth.
My face caressed
By his prickly, blades.
His rich claylike soil
I stroke with my hands.
Soft - burnt like coal.

Rivers of blood flow
Through streaks of lightening...
Silently...yet powerful like
The roars of thunder.
I surrender... myself ...willfully.

This earth of which I'd given birth
Has become my ruler,
My child has become my god.
And now he holds me blame
For a shame that crippled me,
As unwanted as a cancer
That has invaded my bowels
And infected my womb.

He hates me for witnessing his pain.
He thinks my eyes were the
Hands that emasculated him.
When he sees me I strike him
With the portraits of a dynasty crumbled.
Yet I am a reformer.
My mercy yields the renaissance
Of majestic kingdoms

Reborn with the love of self and kind.

He thinks he's become equal because
He eats on marble floors
Willfully cleaning the crumbs
From colonial tables.

He looks at me with disdain.
The soil and dirt upon
My hem reflecting my love
And devotion for him.
My flesh that hugs my bones
Is a mirror for my integrity.
For I still embrace my sun in my plexus (soul)
And my soil in my heart.

My earth will always be my god.
My only fear is that he will not
Accept me when I die.
And I'd had lived better
Never having to been born.

For my purpose in life
Was to lie upon the blades of grass
And nourish the soil with love and companionship,
To raise my head to the heavens
And to always revere my king.

A Man and a Woman

Spawn from the loins,
I've exist in you.
Moon and earth Lord of the orb
Universe you rule.
Dominion is forgotten
Goddess forsaken.
Love cries out, "to thyself be true".

"Remember" the voice speaks within.
Silenced by forced ignorance,
You're beguiled by The Flatterer's dance.
Now you roam man with beast in gas skin.

Nature is despised for the splicing of gene
Spawn from the loin,
I exist for the being.
Supreme in conscious mind.
Divine in pure nectar's vine.

Spawn from the loin
I've exist in you.
We are the beginning of time.

Baby I Don't Wanna Fight

Baby I don't wanna fight.
I want to build you up when
you're down.
I want to lay your head
upon my lap and caress
away your frown.

I will be your rock,
The pillar to support you
When the world is not.
Creating a solution,
Fill in your gaps,
And exercise the love
We both forgot.

The love torn asunder.
When the earth shook and
Roared like thunder.
When the tar covered the scars
Meant to be your shame.
When my womb was invaded
And I was placed the blame.

When the vision of love was
Blinded by the light.
When black became sin,
And white became right.

I just want to love you,
Be a pillar of support.
Because we both know
What we're paying for
Neither one of us bought.

Liberation of the Abused

It's always hard to leave a love.
But like autumn strangles the northern camas
With its fallen leaves
And winter brings in the symbol of death
Crystallizing and smothering life
You have suppressed my growth.

Your idiosyncrasies, an oral scourge
Echoes self-contempt, afraid that I may surpass you.
Your tongue like fist have beaten down
The mental memoirs of doting moments we shared
And abraded them like finely polished marble.

For when we first met, it seemed as if I was
Blinded by your rays of love.
The terrain of our union was covered with
Lilac, honeysuckle, chamomile, sage and camas.

But the cheap scents of synthetic floral and
The musky scent of lime upon your breath
Were harbingers of a changing season?
And I awaken to our love now a vestige in time.

And I escaped you like a slave.
Although my chains have been broken
And my scars are hidden in the hollows of my heart,
I am mentally enslaved by your
Indoctrination of what I could never look like
And what I could never be.

And it is this poison that intoxicates
My potential and maims me as I

Step out into the wilderness trying
To find a place where I belong, looking for acceptance.

But then a gardener, sewing seeds of
Precious fruits of truth, nourished me
As I consumed his food allowing his nectars
To fill me with self-love and freed
Me of self-hate.

And I awake in summer, blossoming in a field
Of sunflowers, running with the wind
Whispering, "I am free,
Free of the coldest season ever".

My Life, My Life, My Life

Upon these pages I jot down my life.
My decisions stretch out like a white line
on old broken and new freshly lain tar roads,
spewed out like never ending ribbons,
beveled in every direction.

The ink bleeds my pains, joys, my highs, my lows,
my blessings, and my woes.

Some times like an oracle its words are omens
that tell me to lay down my pen and live life.

Hmph

Beneath your disdain, pompous contempt and shun of me
Is remiss ignorance that I am as much a part of you
Than any parvenu you consort with.

And the crown upon your head you so polish
Is full of cubic zirconium illusions
That you are greater than me --
Or that your words vibrate on a higher frequency
Just because it takes more effort and time
For the tongue to contort just to speak.
Time I waste not on souls that need a clear vision to be saved.

So while you dress your words in Liberace fabrics
Trying to get standing ovations
I am overturning mental stones
With a language the whole world can overstand.
For a great man once said,
"What man is it that profits if his brother
Is down." (Elijah Muhammand)

I am as less impress with your aerobic oral skills
Than I am anyone that has surpass the ability
to go a day without shitting on themselves
Yet I indulge you still.
'Cuz that's the kind of gal I am.

Walady

Nourish yourself my child.
For once upon a time
These breasts fed the kings and
Queens
Deified as gods and goddesses,
That sat on gold, marble
And alabaster thrones,
And drank from chalice bejeweled
With rubies, diamonds and
Emeralds,
And carried the scepters
Of our royal dynasty,
While voices of the macrocosm
Sung praise to your existence,
And bowed before you
Knowing and not knowing.

Your very presence quaked the cosmos.
Yet behind my mother eyes
You were just a little more than
An involuntary smile --
A flowers response to its gift from the sun.
My love for you blossomed instinctively.

And pain cradled itself
In the shadows of happiness.
For we knew not what may come.
We were but aware that the yang
Possesses the yin in continuity.

Then tumbled the brume upon the stone.
And your throne was cut down in a
Dense, malevolent, squall.

And you remain kings and queens
Once deified as gods and goddesses,
Bound in a smoke screen
Viewing noxious apparitions,
A miasma mentally mutating you
Into the ones to cry out from the fire.

And I cry, for behind the pain
Happiness cradles itself
In the tarnished memoirs
Of gold, marble and alabaster thrones,
And chalices bejeweled with rubies,
Diamonds and emeralds,
And scepters of our royal dynasty.

What was my beginning
May not be your end.
And it pains me to know
That a god created life
While existing in darkness,
And that life will burn
In the light of fire and brimstone
Never knowing gold, marble and alabaster
Thrones and chalices bejeweled
With rubies, diamonds and emeralds,
And scepters of our royal dynasty.

Nourish yourself my child.

As I pray that you drink of my soul,
My love, my memories, my thoughts
My integrity, my honor, my struggle,
My consciousness, my self- love,
My patience and endurance.
And never, never let them take away
Your crown.

Fertile Love

His love was fertile
Sometimes it nourished,
Sometimes it stank like shit.
It always depended on which way the wind blew.

Soul Of The Mayflower

I heard the beat of the drum stop.
I looked around, the children no longer
Danced and hopped.
I looked up and the blue sky turn
Gray with anger.
It wept and its tears cried out danger.

The ocean roared like nothing I heard before.
I saw black faces riding on white horses
Come ashore.
Coming from chariots that floated from
The sea.
Their hands crashed like thunder and
Everyone began to flee.

Someone was struck down by the
Smokeless fire.
"Abioye, Doyo my babies" I cried
As the thunder grew higher.
I grabbed my babies stumbling over
Their brother Bhe-ki-zi-tha.
He was shot by the black faces riding
On white horses speaking the language
Of the people across the river.

We could not understand how could
They consider
To deliver their own brother and sister
Into the hand of the Shaytaan.
Our land destroyed and homes burnt down.
Ifa fell to the ground

And gave birth to Bapoto.
Born amongst the noise as the turmoil
Continued to grow.

"Why, why" I cried as the leather tore into
My flesh.
As they pulled my babies from me
Threw me down and tore my dress.
"Oh Ogun" I shouted as my insides
Were infected and invaded.
But my cries were silence by blows as
The earth faded.

Some fleeing to the deepest part of the
Jungles escaped.
We thought they'd be back to search for
Us at a later date.
I never saw my babies again, never laid them
Across my breast.
We were beaten chained in our own piss,
Feces and hopelessness.

Many cried to Nyambi to come from across
The waters to rescue us.
But no one did. Most of us died and thrown
Overboard because it was too many of us.
I didn't think I was to make it myself
Having lost so much weight.
I shivered until I could no longer, the flesh
Falling off my waist.

As I laid in my stool with sores from the
Filth head to toe.

Some ate their feces because not enough
White stuff around to go.
My lips blistered and tongue raw, my flesh
Opened with illness and sores.
Each one was filled with sugar and tar
Burning flesh to the core.

My throat burnt like fire and almost closed shut
My mind kept tracing back to our village
And my family's hut.
Every night they came to me tearing into
My private parts.
They beat my man in front of me hoping
He would lose my heart.

I tried to escape and run back to the river
Hoping a boat would carry me across the
Sea back to freedom.
After the third time they cut my leg off
But even that didn't stop them.

They could take away my dignity and make
Me bear their seed.
For even in foiled soil I can still fertilize
The dill weed.

And I knew I would never see my home again,
No never again.
Lost in this strange wilderness wishing
My life would soon end.

For only in death will we find the answers why
As for now, I am but flesh whose soul from
The mayflower continues to cry.

Time Out

When I was a youth and I birth truth,
All I wanted to do was warn people.
"You must wake up to the truth
Because we are running out of time."
My concern was that many will not know
The truth before it was too late,
Before *we* ran out of time.

Now I am older --
And I realize,
The only time I see running out
Is mine.

And I realize how much time I wasted
Not cherishing the time I had
In my time of youth.

So now I spend my time in truth,
Knowing that I need time for me --
Time to open my mind to the time that I have --
And the space to do so many things I missed,
Worrying about something that does not move.
For time stands still --
We just travel through time,
From the beginning of one segment
To the end of another.

So now I occupy my space in time
With the things that make me happy --
Until my space in time dissipates.
Now I shout...
"It's time I take time out for me."

Execrable Soul

Take no mind to enter my realm of confusion --
For it is like liquid, and you may quickly be submerged.
I, myself, seek refuge from my fears,
But they haunt me like the stench that wafts the
City's dump, and stings my mind with a pungent
Reality.

Today the pride I had in my family was defused by
News that my brother 48 cannot even take care of
Himself.
Another strike against my soul
And I am forming hopeless notions that I may be the
Vessel to foster the state of deficiency that exist
In the dimension of my progenitors.
I who has worn pessimism as a brand like Cain,
In hopes that I would be spared burdens to
Great for me to bear.

Yet it appears I am afflicted with the responsibility
To purge my genetics from this lethargic curse
With a DNA explosion of consciousness, coinciding
With the concentrated effort of an execrable soul
To believe I in fact can succeed.

Fools Go Where Angels Fear To Tread

You have treaded on this earth
Over a quarter of a century --
And where exactly have you taken me?
Running in the wind like scattered leaves
You've settled so many places,
Yet you've never remained steadfast.

I've circled the iron with you,
Yet still skilled at many and master at none.
What can you tell the needy?

Twenty seven moons and you've fallen twenty five feet
Into what can lead you into an abyss.
Yet you continue to circle the cave
Because its echoes resonate such sweet sounds.
Its vibrations are hypnotic
And spins you around and around and around
Until your ears are ringing
And you can hear no other sound.

And although you relish these echoes
That call out in the hollowness of your existence,
You know that the day will come

When the cave will crumble --
And there will be no further calls --
No accolades in the wind --
No caressing of vibrations.
There will be but silence.

And you will once again
Take me on the path that fools take --
Watching the people of promise abscond you.
For you constantly travel the desert of endless sand
And the wind whispers contemptibly in your ear,
"Will you ever learn? Will you ever find your way?"

Waste Not Want Not

How delicate and fragile
Are my fleeting thoughts and epiphanies.
For if I treasure them not with caution
They shall dissipate in my mind like vapors.

And the energy of my contemplations
Are shared in the mental reservoir.
The seeds of my creativity are carried
On the wings of the efficient
To sow fruition in a vessel of prosperity.

And I am left empty with a hole in my fate
Futilely pouring thoughts within.

Mind Travel

There is nothing strange about
Traveling through the psyche.
What matters is what you get
Out of sojourning in that thought.

Can your mind's eye be honest enough
To see truth in the abode you linger?
Do you learn how to avoid the detours
Giving you a bum steer --?
Or are you constantly taking southeast turns
Into cotton candy illusion and chocolate coated lies,
Because the abode of truth
Is as desolate as a ghost town, or
A torrid desert?

It is virtually impossible to find someone
that is willing to dwell there with you.

Do you sometimes feel isolated from truth,
who is the correction officer
that keeps putting you in solitary confinement?
So you plea for a pardon of truth so that you
can celebrate calumniation, hypocrisy,
delusion and illusions.

The truth is a bitter tonic that cures lies,
cataracts and reveals every one of your stones
unturned, too many to cast.

Can You Hear the Beat

No one knows my song,
Yet it has played in my head
For twenty nine years.

When I first heard it,
It was as beautiful as a wedding song --
And I felt like the bride of truth.

Every so many years the song
Was revised, and like a bad remake
I began to lose favor for the song --
Wishing the old tune would replay.
But it was put away, replaced by a new.

Now this song plays like a mantra in a
Séance that conjures up nothing but pain.
And all these years it has played I alone
Know it.
As deafening as it is to me, I alone
Hear it.

You have no idea how the song
Of my life goes.
And I in a million years could never hum
Out the tune to make you hear.
For even if I tried,
You couldn't understand its beats.

And for this reason I move through life
Performing the dance of the enchanted
In a spell cast by my soul until...

Warrior with No Worth

Wasted warriors shouting words
Or warnings with no works --
As useless as the rebel with no cause.

You throw punches with no limbs
Trying to strike the world.

For if you show no example
Than your shouts are whispers,
And the still wind cannot hear you.

Your spirit is as strong as water is to venom.
It only waters down the poison
But encumbers it not.

The only war you win
Is the disillusion over reality.
For you consume worthlessness
As if it is nutrients,
And think you will form spiritual muscles.

You are as dense in matter
As a jewel filled with useless alloy.

So speak the truth
But don't think your words
Will afford you worth
To reign with the Lamb.

For the true warriors
Are suffering in the field --
And it is for them the rapture
Shall come.

The Gene of Myself

Like Sabriya,
My soul has turned to salt with no savor.
The Lot of my land imprisoned,
Now wishes to return home

Immortal dreams die a second death
As walls fall in promised flames.
Yet I continue to write
Disillusioned that this will alter cursed genetics.

Each stroke I pour out my soul
As I foolishly pour out my soul --
Leading others down shallow amber paths.

I see visions of self- destruction
Plasmatic images -- apparitions of a future.

I've walked for decades in a hypnotic trance.
Seduced by Delilah, I stand a broken souljah,
Beneath the pillars of a crumbling Philistine temple.
And I stretch out my arms welcoming my fate.

For it is I that have allowed
My locs of righteousness to be cut --
And refuse to grow them upon a betrayer.

I seek refuge from myself --
And the whisperings of myself --
And the gene or jinn of myself.

Just Another Love Poem

I smelt the scent of spring approaching
In the morning dew
And I thought about waking up to you

The fragrance of my flower
Blossoming in the slight parting of your lips
The essence I willfully submitted
With the parting of my hips.

The forecast rain
Each sparkling iridescent drop I taste,
Each moment shared with you --
It beats upon my windowpane

It summons the rhythm of your heart,
When it was just us two listening to jazz,
Crackling fires, and inhaling the scent
Of cedar floors.
All open the corridors
To memoirs of the one I adore.

And I long for the touch of your lips,
For that kiss that seems to stop
The measuring of time and space
And that moment is made indelible in existence --
It will never be erased.

There is a kindred here –
Molecules aggregated into one love - you and I
And I will long for you in each beaching tide --

Each stroke of the wind --
With each rising and setting of the sun --
Look for you in every silhouette and haven
From the beckoning moon,
In each twinkling of the stars.
And I will find you every night
In the solitude of my heart,
Remembering the scent
Of your flower between your thigh
The feel of you, the taste of you
Until the day I die.

He Must Be Kidding

He tried to say I still had feelings for him.
I pondered what feelings that would be.

Like feeling a scar from a healed chickenpox --
The twitching of a chicken after his head's been cut off.

That dull ache every once in a while where a tooth used to be --
That thought of prison an ex con has every now and then
My uterus contracting when nursing, reminding me of labor

Hm, yes you're right. I still have feelings for you.
Psst. (walking away mumbling,)
Asshole

Spectrum of Love and Life

Blue skies
Yellow smiles
Diamond tears
Emerald emotions
Ruby glares
Red lust
Black love
Brown caresses
Indigo nights
Purple passion
Amber stimulations
Orange kisses
Pink labia
Hot pink licks
Chocolate pricks
Iridescent climaxes
Ivory orgasms
Silver dreams
Golden realities
Spectrum of life and love

Submissive Whore

Have you've awaken alone
With a thousand loves
Loving you for what you can give,
While your cup remains empty?

Like a star on stage
Tossed a myriad of roses
But no one knows your real name
Or even your favorite color.

Stuck in a world of their needs,
While you are consumed with
An insatiable famine --
Hoping someone will give
You that food for thought
You hunger for.

That one you adore can sup with --
Feeding you eloquent cuisines
With hotplates that emit
Aphrodisiac steam.

Have you ever been loved
By many but have never
Felt so alone?

In a world of no reciprocity
How can I feel their love?

Yet they want what they want

And foolishly think I want the same --
Cursing me for not appreciating
Their love.

So like a cheap whore. I fake it.

Second Degree Murder

Co-defendant --
Bartered life
For death.

Became a conspirator
To harbor hate.

Raising it,
With each blow,
Life was expelled.

And there it lay
On the floor --
In a puddle
Of my bloody
Expectorant

The end
Of my --

Love.

July Skies in Sumner

Maple syrup drip dreams
Down my ruffle sleeves.
Hazy window pass times
Pondering if I had to fly
Seven stories to the ground.

Blazing ships the elders call Hinu
Now have earthly explanations,
Hidden by July skies -- dotted by
Liberty's torch --
Or that state's pen in the sky --
High,
Lit up like a bomb pop.

And it frightens me to elevate there.
For fear I'll be trapped
In the pedophile's killer box
Pandora to past pain.

And I keep hearing the sounds
Of strawberry fields in twenty three keys,
Written on sodden walls
Based by turkeys with chemical libations

Wondering why dogs howl in circles
When there were no reported deaths.
In this valley where the dead walk

And the black and blue leave
Their signature on my skin

Raised in the wind
When you party in Billy's club.
You always see stars brighter than that
Bomb pop in the sky on July nights.

And I awake on the other side of time.

Cain Smote Abel

The walls are thinner now,
Since he threw that punch.

My heart sinking because
It was I who put the force
In his fist
And the temper in his heart.

Now the walls are mocking me
For my genetic influences.
And I lie in my bed
Afraid of the beat of each step
For fear the final scuffle will break

And their room is a temperate battle zone
Where he should be seeking support
And protection
He has to live in fear of the next strike
And the consequences of his retaliation.

And my soul is tormented
By the thinning of the walls.

Fuse My Lips So Words Cannot Escape

She cradles knowledge in her existence
Like possessing condoms in a world of infidels
Bludgeoned by invisible stones.

Their obtuse rigidness tearing into her heart,
Peeling away the layers of her world,
Until she remained alone in a box,
With painted on realities --
Trying to conjure up life from the dead,
Just so she could have someone to talk to --
Someone that shared her secrets.

NyQuil gel caps consumed daily.
And although the writing is clear,
They ignore its affects
Walking in a mental repose,
Falling into ditches.

And she spins around and around and around
In a kaleidoscope of consciousness
Sick as a dog --
Hoping one day this ride will stop,
And she'd be let off in a land where
She'd feel free to be she.

Until that day,
She'll stand on the podium,
In the center of the city
Signing futilely
Ominous words to the blind.

Sweet Sadie

The Old English man stole you momma
Stole the arms and breast that kept me warm
Took away the memories before his invasion
Now just see curled up decadence
And drunken dreams

Can't remember stories you told
I told stories to my children
But the beatings probably stole them away.

I wasn't as good a mother as you momma
Not at first
But I tried to be better.

Still haven't met anyone as beautiful as you
Except for my baby
He is loving just like you
Down to the mole on his eye.

Sorry I left you momma
Sorry I rejected you.
Will you reject me when it's my time

I am almost embarrassed to see you again
Have I shamed you momma
Told too many truths
In my effort to survive losing you

Think I've gone a little crazy since
You left momma.
Been looking for you in others

Just to hold you again
To feel your love again.

Feel I'll see you soon momma
Although I hope you are at rest
Forgive me for the casket
Thought about ashes to ashes
Dust we shall return.

Have not been to the grave yet momma
But I know you are no longer there
I pray you are at rest momma
Think I might see you soon
Seems the good go that way
Maybe not ornery enough to stay

Tired anyway
But hope I see you again momma
Like I saw you in my dream
Didn't play the number
you gave me momma
570 came out three times,
three different ways

Sometimes I feel
like a motherless child momma
So far away from home.
Think I'm going a little crazy momma
Tired of being alone.
Good night Momma
Sweet Sadie
I love you.

A Tree's Life

This tree's leaves
Still somewhat green
Are beginning to fall,
As her limbs grow limp.

The cipher of her life
Shows no wisdom --
Just a fool's mistakes
And lessons learned too late.

The earth parts beneath her feet
And her fruits have fallen
Onto the dank soil beneath her.

Separated from the rest of her orchard
She stands naked to the sun,
Scorched by life.

Her burns slowly wounding her,
She contemplates a bitter end,
That one day she may be struck down.

Her only fear is in what way
Shall her fruit be consumed.
Her regrets
Are in how she allowed herself
To be misused
As the innocent
Hung from her limbs.

Life Please

I love the sound of letters from A to Z.
I love the way the rain falls upon me.

The sky shines brightly through the clouds.
No complaint is too loud.

Hope is in the vertical and mobile.
The vagabond is king and the whore is noble.

War is a task absent the right solution.
I shun the monk living in seclusion,
Absconding chaos bond by religious trepidation,
Afraid of falling prey to temptation.

For this little woman weeps for life.
The Most High made the world my
Husband and experience is his wife.

It is the least bias in all existence.
It breeds like the evergreen in winter's solstice.

As the snow numbs the tips of my fingers
I am reminded that His love for me lingers.

For I will not take my sabbatical this day.
I will ride the high tide and leave death at bay

And I will eschew the sun upon my horizontal
And learn to love breath sippin' on Cristal

The Baron of Strawberry Fields

There's a greedy ass mogul that's reached its vantage point.
The one God and the devil both anoint.
Controlling people with his obscurities.
Pushing people to the edge for righteous name sake.
And all he does is take, take and take.

And I just can't take this shit any more.
Pimping people like a pimp does a whore,
With his flashing lights, bright
Down white corridors.

Passing through life got people all fucked up,
Wondering when he's gonna give them his cup.
Acting all mystical got souls wondering --
Pondering --
Laundering intentions
Squandering their precious time away
Clinging on to chaos just to keep him at bay.

No one's ever came back from visiting him to say.
"Hey this MoFo is really okay.
He's on the level,
As long as you ain't selling your soul to the devil."

All he does is sit back and revel
At his wealth.
Snatching people's health.
Dwelling in stealth -- mode.
He's a cold motherfucker... He's so, so cold.

And behold

Multitudes stand at his door.
Yet this greedy mogul,
Just wants more and more and more.

Most powerful in all the world.
He'd even rape a little boy or girl,
Take their life before it barely had a chance
Like a callous colonial taking what's not his,
And then performing a victory dance.

How many martyrs got to pay him their life?
Hasn't he seen enough strife --?
Seen enough flesh fall of the bone,
Enough sacrifice before his thrown
As they call him home?
The world is his capital zone.
Why doesn't he leave us the hell alone?

Please hear my plea.
You see, this is the key,
If you can just tone down your spree
To a certain degree,
Then just maybe... just maybe
I can be free --
Free to live another day,
Free to right the wrongs and the goings astray
Free to... to... to... just...
Can I just finish a few books?
Maybe just one okay.
Just shut down your all you can take buffet
So I can just...
Just... Please Death --
Please don't take me this way.

Africa

I've never been to Africa,
but it's starting to feel like home.
I ain't never been to Africa,
but I bet it feels like home.

These dark shadow of beings,
seeking mendacious dreams,
from milk and honey fiends --
leaving, fleeing, believing,
going through unbelievable extremes --
anything to fulfill that pipe dream.

And I'm grieving   --   lost -- no control
So many boldly selling their souls.
Diamonds covered in coal.
Ignorance grows waxed cold.
Behold, unfolds the lies they told.

Now lost in this wilderness,
digress and under duress --
stressed, depresse, and must confess,
I ain't supposed to be in this mess.

And I've never been to Africa
but it's starting to feel like home.
I ain't never been to Africa
but I bet it feels like home.

Travel down tarred roads at night.
these wooden walls closing in tight.
Speaking no one hears my plight.
I fight to write I might make it right.
My insight block by white knights

battling to keep 9 ether inferior.
Canine malpose anterior
gnashing smashing mirrors.
Reflections of truth no longer clearer.
Ulterior motives to look superior.
Worshipping gods with pale exteriors.
Mother superior and mother of god.
Peacemaking killing squads,
try to rule with iron teeth and rods.
Now I wander in this land of Nod,
Because this land's starting to feel odd.

And I've never been to Africa,
but it's starting to feel like home
I ain't never been to Africa
but I bet it feels like home.

Living in the belly of the beast,
vomiting up his disease --
walking in shadows of the decease.
My freedom's shacked on a leash.
Priest conjure, unleash, necromancy feast.
I am to say the least the platter,
beguiled with promises and flatter.

Goals shatter, everything that matters
scattered by false chatter... his story.
Set me free to see my-story
beyond rubber trees and thrones of glory
from the banks of the Nile and Euphrates.

Your stories bores me -- because
it's not for me. Gods we be --
cause your life has flaws.
I can't live by your laws.
Just 'cause, just cause...Just-Us does

Our sisters and brothers no justice.

We exist like hoecakes
And blackstrap molasses,
Stuck in a folktale mental abyss.
And I'm piss, because I reminisce.
This I miss - that sweet land of bliss

And I've never been to Africa,
But it's starting to feel like home.
I ain't never been to Africa
But I bet it feels like home.

Black Girl

Black Girl, Black Girl,
Whatchu crying for?
Because you aren't what
The brothers adore?
With your wide ass nose
And your bubba lips.
What about you makes you think
You should be the one
The brothers kiss?

When I look at you, I hate you
Because you remind me
Of a suffering and inferiority
Of what it means to be me.

So why should I tote you on my
Arm, treat you good?
Shit you belong on my mother's
mantle piece decorating
her piano in wood --
with big ass holes in your ears,
and rings around your neck.
You're a Jigaboo that
the whole world rejects.

Except for the motherland
where I was kidnapped away.
Shit I'm still wearing the scars
from that day.
So if I go back then I'll take you,
but that ain't for a while.
'Cuz right now I'm in white America

and you ain't in style.

Agatha, Agatha, skin as black
as the velvety skies.
Baary Baary White!
Pupils black as maidens,
With the pathway to the past
In the whites of your eyes,
Leading me to a doorway
To the soul I must sell to survive.
Believing the lies... believing the lies.
White is right, black stay back.
Step on a crack,
Break your mother's back.

Black Girl, Black Girl
How dare you remind me
Of the pain of wanting
To love the image of me,
And being mentally
And physically free.
Do you have the answers,
Black Girl, Black Girl,
To the troubles of this
Blackman's world?

'Cuz right now all I can see,
The answer to relieving
this pain in me, is the unity
Of the Blackman's mentality.
I've watched many martyrs die
Struggling toward that
Utopian fantasy.
So don't dare judge me,

if I cannot see.

For as a slave in this
mis-educated freedom,
I am forced to conform
to his kingdom.
For only in the Blackman's
mental freedom,
shall I truly find
God's kingdom, come.

Perish Not My Love

Can she love the soul of me?
Bare as a dare, fresh, fearless and vibrant...
Vulnerable, exposed and free.

It is the essence of love,
That life force that fashions the smile
In the abyss, and invokes joy.

It's translucent and purer than matter.
For ultimately it's the only thing that matters,
When the phases of life brings us closer
To our end...

And agility is trapped in images of illusions
Once realities
Yet, the impressions of my love
Remain eternal,
Incessant, luminous rings
Interwoven and elapsing throughout
Each segment of our
Journey towards holism...
Where vowels are syncopated,
And consonants choked by the visceral will.

This love, this priceless
Unfettered love,
Will she treat like the avaricious...?
Ignoring the blessing
Of nature to choke down
Inebriates and toxins

To define their worth --
Who love with hidden desires?

My love is virtuous
But will she ever come to know it?
As it lays there before her feet,
Will she let it whisk her away?
Or shall she tread upon my eternal love
For that which perishes?

Brooklyn Blues

Like an abuser
In search of his lover -- mumbling
"Which way... which way...
It's blades slice into the sky.

Beaming lantern sway to and fro
Marching down celestial corridors.
Sirens scream out as if wailing women
Were absconding their predators

Flashing blue and white
Are the strobe lights
For the dance of death

Street side sorcerers conjure nostalgia --
Burning water chestnut love potions,
That seep into my soul –
And I find myself in a hypnotic trance --
Wandering in a concrete jungle.

My diffidence
Are exposed before the charlatan --
Nipples bare –
Harder than ripe blackberries,
And just as sweet
Caressing prisms the moon cast from above
Penetrating my bay windows.

I am that princess
And only my iron lover can save me

With one bite of that sensual, eclectic,
Eccentric, provocative and amoral apple.
And I awake free of moral sutras
On a jaunt towards decadence --
Never feeling more alive
As poignant stench of gunpowder
Burns my nose,

He Berates me -- stinging my ears.
The cold chill of my impersonal lover
Passes me by.

And I smile
Needing his unattached love
That swallows me whole.

And as I inhale the scent of cedar,
I exhale happiness,
For I know my estrange lover
Has welcomed me home.

Renaissance Woman

Her strength is her gift.
It transcends instinctively.
Yet who is she who finds the right man
In this strength.

For at times its image is plagiarized
By aggression and dominance.
And many men are lost in the matrix,
Leaving a strong woman alone with
Her love caught up inside.

This Renaissance woman is complex,
But her love is simple.
When she loves, like everything she does
She loves hard.
'Tis why, when she hurts, she hurts hard.
Often life feeds her gall --
And relationships rise and fall.

She's not partial to weak men
And is a threat to the strong --
Too ignorant to see possessing
Her is priceless,
The most precious jewel
In the world.
For her very presence
Illuminates his strength

Therefore I say,
Stand strong Renaissance woman --

And love with an I'll be damned
Kind of love.

And if they can't understand it,
Then fuck'em... fuck them.
Until you find the one that does.

Soul Food Blues

I'z be blessed
Been eating watermelon for 400 years I guess;
Black eye peas, yams, chitlins, all that mess.
Boil out all the shit and I confess
It taste just as good as the rest.
I thinks it taste the best.

Woo, had to cook for Ms. Lady
And the lot of her'n family.
Now that tooks a lot out of me.
Theyz ain't eat what weez eat though
Theyz eat choice beef don'tchu know.
Theyz eat vegetable like spinach, broccoli
And asparagus.
Theyz don't even puts fat back in it likes the
Rest of us.

Theyz so snowy white and soft to speaks of
Likes silk or the fur of a dove
Howz can theyz begin to love
My rough hands --
Flesh thick as pressed leather,
Carved and cut up
And beaten by the weather

Mistah's eyes is on me though
I'z thinks he taken a liken, I don't know
I'z can lose myself if'n I don't watch out
Lose the ugly I'z feel and theyz talk about

My chilren a have the chance to be stand
Keeps this up theyz chilren a be the man
Theyz hair be good and chin held high
Got no problem lookin' you in the eye

No worries with theyz hair.
I tell you 'tis just ain't fair.
Whyz we end up with the curse?
Pssht, and my granddaddy say we came first.

Seems like if that be'n true
Then weez be the one tellin' e'rbody
Else what to do.

Sometimes I feelz like I'z got no mammy
Or pappy, let alone God.
If he love me so much how come he
Love me with a whip and rod?

Shit in that case Mistah's God all the way.
Get introduce to him three and four times a day --
Just fixin' my tongue to form words to say,
I don't think in your bed I wants to lay.

Even if I said that it wouldn't be true.
Truth is there's nothing I won't do --
To erase the shame, the pain
The hate, sadness and gloom.
Because as far as I'z concern,
Without the Whiteman weez be doomed.

Wonder what's more detrimental

Racisms or inferiority, fed by the colonial
The deliberate attack to the mental.

Racism may be a blow with a Billy stick
But inferiority keeps you in fear of it
And doing something to change it.

Randy

My mouth is stuffed with empty kisses
And I swallow empty wishes
As my thoughts ejaculate inside me
And wet me with its ecstasy
Squirting manifestations of a dream.

My desires are a flowing stream
Of peaches and cream
And I cross over into a land
Where the natives have surnamed me Randy

The Strength of a Woman

She lights the world up from the sun of her smile.
Beneath the surface it burns her like fire.
She stays strong constantly holding on --
Because she has to.

No, she cannot walk away from the legacy dealt her;
The butcher, the baker, the candlestick maker,
Lover, mother, sometimes farther, she becomes a father.
And you wonder why she chooses happiness
From whoever brings it --
Irregardless of your judgmental eye.

So she walks with the wind of contempt against her,
Using her as a vulnerable target,
Tearing into her soul like the stinging,
Gushing winds of Mid-Manhattan,
In the heart of the winter solstice.
She tolerates its coldness just the same,
As wounds begin to open.

But there lies warmth in self-assurance,
Self-love and the resolution to decide --
"I'm gonna take a vacation into the Jamaica,
And Bahamas of me --
Open the articles of my heart and say fuck it.
My time to think of me
And do what it takes to make me happy."

Fire in Their Eyes (For Troy Davis)

Cries for justice spew out
Like roaring thunder unto the heavens,
But its ears have grown deaf.

And the wicked will once again
Destroy hope
As the innocent becomes
But a statement to a Blackman --
That he is still less
In this chalky wilderness,
That has become
A diaspora of presidential ignorance,
A cultural decadence
And diatribe on freedom,
Justice and equality.

Innocence is not the fight.
No, this war is waged to maintain
A hierarchy of oppression,
For all which they have stolen
And murdered to possess.
In this pale, bloodless, waxed cold wilderness.

And the people of the world
Eyes burn like flames of fire,
As they look into the future
Of their existence --
Rummaging through
The receipts of their past --
Trying to find that one they can return

For their sold integrity, souls,
Consciousness, and conscience --
In hopes that it will barter them mercy,
As the last spectrum bends the sky,
And the flames from the hell they made
With the brush of their careless hands
And the turn of their docile cheeks
Reflect from their damned eyes.

We are cursed
To see the final judgment
Of our own lack of fortitude,
And lose of determination.
For we've closed our eyes on the struggle.

Castration of Love

Baby can you sit down and let me talk to you for a bit.
Look, I just want to talk to you for a minute.
Because I am trying to figure out
A way to stop loving you.
Baby I can't stay here with you
And continue to go through
The things that we go through.

And I've been trying
To wrap my mind around this situation --
Because honestly, although I love you dearly,
I can't continue to go through these frustrations.

I know, I know, 'for God
You have never lain a single hand on me.
But I don't know what's worse,
The physical abuse
Or the pains of living with these insecurities

Baby, don't you know you are making it so hard
For me to serve you --
And that's all I ever really wanted to do.
But my heart and my soul is full of so much turmoil --
And I don't care how much you I love or spoil,
You continue to take me for granted --
Disrespect me and behave underhanded,
While all the time feeding me you double standards --

And I can't stand it -- being a victim.
Wondering when the time will come

When you'll decide to destroy the commitment
We've made to one another.
So right now, I see you like a serial killer --
Slaughtering the love of the innocent
And moving on to the next sucker.

Like a butcher --
You've trimmed the meat from this relationship
And I sit here trying to figure out
Is it worth struggling to stay afloat, or should I just jump ship --
Before you kill me.
Because frankly,
I don't know to what degree
You've been cheating on me.

But I know, right now, I'm passed the nights
Of wanting to end it all --
Wondering when I will receive your call
Telling me you're coming in late.
And I can't continue to make these redundant mistakes

Or believe I can get back the man
I was willing to do whatever it took
Just to make him smile.
The man I prayed to God
For a chance to conceive his child --
Just to duplicate
What I thought was a God personified.
But like Alpha and Omega,
Thanks to you, the love that was alive, has now died.

And although I may be a fiend for your very being --

And I just may very well be addicted to your frame --
I can't continue to play these fools games

It's been a painful journey, but I've finally arrived.
You see, I can be without you
And still survive.
I've come to terms
That I can actually do better without you --
Because I've come to terms
That I love me and as long as I do,
I won't have a problem finding someone better
To replace you.
Please, please don't contort your tongue
To tell me she didn't mean anything to you.
Like that's the golden response
That would make me consider staying with you.
All it shows is your ill regard
And disrespect for women
And that is not the kind of influence
I want to expose to my children.

So I'm leaving you,
With the house, the business you turned to ruins
And yes, the Benz
Because frankly, I have all I need.
I have my faculties, my ability to succeed and achieve
And my children
So step away from the door
Because I don't want you,
I don't need you,
And I don't love you anymore.

'Tis Why I went to the other side

How dare you question me why.
When I longed for you, you passed me by
Not even blinking an eye.
The beauty you now see in me,
Was only discovered with the reality
Of his adoration of me.

I would have given my life for you,
Because my soul is for you,
And I know the completion of me is in you.

But I cried at your feet,
And my heart pleaded with you every day --
And you treaded upon my love,
As I watched the footprints in the sand carry you away.

And while I bowed to you,
Praying you saw the beauty in me --
I smelt the sweet scent of roses he cast at my feet,
Adoring and worshipping the image of me

And my heart ached, because the someone that
Loved me was not you.
So with the need to be loved and without further ado --
I allowed his love for me to replace the love I felt for you.

To replace the ugly I felt and the disgrace,
When a brother behind me would gawk at my ass
Beautifully toned legs and body,
Then turn away when he saw my face,

Because I wasn't light or damn near white --
Or because my nose was too wide or lips to full
For you to forget that the ugly and self-hate
That you have in you.

Living by the white America's indoctrination of beauty --
Not their standard of beauty.
Because this white man's standard of beauty is me
With my full lips, wide nose, big ass, dark tone
And yes, all of my sexualities.

You see, I used to care about what you thought –
But not anymore.
Because while you are judging me,
I'm being his consummate mother whore.

I spent thirty years of my life
Following religious moralities and living in submission
Had me faced down on the ground
With a loaded AK at my head and back
About to die for the mission
Until I realize morality
Is a tool for the elite to control the meek --
When I found out that all the saints in my life
Were sinners and freaks.

So while you hold your white girl on your arm,
That will do all the things a sistah won't --
Don't sit there and trying to judge and dictate to me
My fucking does and don'ts.
I am a woman in full bloom with her sexuality.
And he accepts and pleases me with an exigency

That ignites the very depth of me.

Because frankly --
If you're not having sex for the biblical reasons,
Then all you motherfuckers are in holy treason.

So I'm gonna get my freak on
Without any inhibitions or labels
That's right --
I'll take it sensual, consensual
From whoever brings it to the table.
And you can put whatever label you want on it.
Because as far as I'm concerned, fluid is fluid.

So I'm not going to sit in a closet,
Because you refused to take in all the benefits of me --
When I have someone who adores me --
And lays it down without any sexual or erotic inhibitions.
Because you see, in his life, I'm his mission.

And although I love me to death
Some beautiful black men --
That waiting on you to recognize the beauty in me
Has come to an end
There will be no intermittence here
You see, this squirrel will get her nut this year.

From Whence I Get My Corn

My mind is constantly torn
From whence I get my corn.
You see, I know what's important,
I am aware of the cause and struggle --
But the passion inside of me is
Caught up in a bubble.

And although I know he is my king and
I his queen,
I can't lose this underlying feeling,
And the need to liberate myself
Constantly revealing this energy
Imploding inside.

You see, I know where society says I belong
Is by his side --
And for this nation to generate gods of hope --
Well it behooves me to abide.

And please, please don't get me wrong --
My love for him is forever strong.
Why Heqet I be --
Instilling the spark of life to he,
Who brings it back to me,
Birthing a genesis of conscious gods we see,
Black and comely as the tents of Kedar --
By no means inferior by far,
Because I see the regal beyond the scar

That mental wound he tars

With lily white love --
That needs to feel substantiated
He can't seem to get rid of.

For when he looks at me,
He can't forget the whip that stripped pride
And integrity and bruised lips --
Equipped with enough shame
To place the blame upon my raped hips --

Ashamed of the pain of loving self and kind.
Being targeted, hunted, shackled
And imprisoned scars his mind.

And being that goddess
That sees the divine being in you,
I just can't accept anything less
Than that glory from you --
From paper bag bright brothers to black as blue.

Yet and still,
I find myself drawn to the kinship
I speak unspoken --
With a black woman raised from a life
That's been broken.

The educator, butcher, baker,
Candlestick maker, mother and even lover --
A force to be reckon with like no other
No one is sympathetic to her job
That's goes undone.

Her strength can be compared to none.

So when I see the symmetric beauty,
That I behold in front of me,
I can't ignore the need,
Nor the nagging exigency
To shower her with accolades
In an oral escapade.
I fade into the cascades
Of her curves and bevels --

Burrowing into her vortex in so many levels
Nourishing myself, consuming the knowledge
Of 360 degrees I pledge
Allegiance to the mysteries wedged
Between her thighs and on I dredge
In search for the essence of everything in me
That makes me a woman, the epitome
Of creation
That fifth element and mother of all nations

So you see, loving both gods and goddesses
Is not just a carnal greed
It's a pure and essential requisite that I need
To digress from the cultural decadence
In a Diaspora of ignorance
And reunite self-love, appreciation,
Culture and kinship
That was stolen from me
With a physical and mental whip
That stripped pride and integrity
And bruised lips --

Equipped with enough shame
To place the blame upon my raped hip

And so now --
Now I have the fortitude to say --
Fuck you in every way.

Fuck your arbitrary laws
That exonerates your wrong
And commits me to sin
Moralizing everyone else
While basking in your wicked predilections
Irregardless of your bias doctrine
Nothing can take the place
Of the experience I get from
Beautiful black and comely Nubian men...and
....and yes women.

Fake Ass Civil Right Leaders

Struggles in the thirties to the seventies go unheard today.
Basking in martyred blood, but when we need a voice, fake ass
civil rights leaders ain't got shit to say.
Puppet side show freaks with crocodile tears screaming equality.
When it's time to really make a change they turn their backs
easily.
They fight for fake causes to make a name for themselves.
Motherfuckers only care about money and fame. They don't give
a shit about anyone else.

Coal covered diamond sold their souls a long time ago.
From ride or die soldiers to hold de do' dead black Negros.
You see, the scheme is the devil buys these agents to lead you
astray.
Making you think they're down for the struggle, but really they
ain't got shit to say.
Liberace words and show boating with no substance.
And in the back of their minds they're saying, "these niggas ain't
got a chance"

They are all just a part of the devil's plan
To set you back 80 years into that age of ignorance.
Took you 40 years to even say black is beautiful.
Brought you from American Negro to African American, no
longer a foot stool.
Now you act like it's shameful to be cultural.
Let him put your Nubian women at the base of the totem pole.

I ain't never heard a white man call his white woman a bitch, ho or
slut in an everyday conversation.

124

But will hear a brother say it with elation --
Like a trained negro off the plantation --
Taught to hate his Nubian queen and foundation,
Forgetting she's the mother of our Nubian nation.

You frown at the use of the word Coloreds
But have no problem accepted the term People of Color
If you can't see that's the same damn thing
then your intellect has regressed even smaller
Back to exalting that lily white image
and Nubians are stumbling to ride that white horse.
Done fell off the course with no remorse

So blinded by the bling-bling
Can't see the devil's making evil fare seeming
Can't you see he is working from every aspect
to keep you from connecting to who you really are?
Damn can't you see he is chopping down everything we built to get
this far.

All the black leaders are either dead or in jail without bail.
Killing the soul in the music sneaking in destructive rock with his
C note without fail
Now everybody's got to bling-bling with the designer ho flow
Care more about the material then your spiritual, physical and
mental growth.
COENTELPPRO left you with no one to remind you of your worth.
Motherfuckers have you forgotten the growth of your nation
comes first.

You see the problem is the devil plans for the future of his nation
While Nubians plan for self-glorification.

We've lost the leaders with the integrity and insight willing to die for our nation to grow.
All we got are these fake ass civil rights side show freak Negros.
Making it harder for the real soldiers to be heard
So their cries are like pages of justice with no words.

The black devil is the most detrimental to our race.
That's why we no longer have His grace.
We've forgotten our course, our integrity, our goals
And His wrath is going to continue to unfold --
Because unfortunately, the only time you remembered to struggle, is when you were being abused, oppressed, and had no voice.
So don't cry out when this comes to pass, because he answered your prayers, and gave you your reign, and now you're just tap dancing it away to the devil by choice.

And I'm pissed, because I reminisce and refuse to dismiss my integrity my love for self and my divinity.
He will never take that crown from me,
Like you allowed him to take it from you
Side show, fake ass, civil right, fraud, dead black, American Colored Negro

Ye Are Gods

Alas the saints rape the sinners
Of their righteousness
Speaking babbles of an unholy ghost.
For the disciples of the Holy Spirit
Spoke clear for all nations to understand
And hear it.

Yet we're left dumfounded --
Confounded
By that gastation you called God's host
God being that "g" in ghost –
For the Most --
Most High is Supreme
And according to his word
The father of that god being --

For ye are gods and all of ye
Are the children of the Most high
And it is for that principle you should live and die
That is your constitution made by God
And you should not be swayed by peacemaking killing squads

So we walk with that divinity
In a mental trance.
For the darkness knows not the light
When the devil flaunts finance.
Looking for riches in owed dollars and cents --
While shuffling and signifying,
Doing the latest minstrel dance.
And you wonder why Nubians ain't got a chance.
Because they lack the fortitude
To resist ignorance.

And the man that knows something
knows that he knows nothing at all.
Yet this I know --
That while I was in the love of the all
An angel from heaven was taking a fall
And as I look around I realized all
The true leaders only exists on walls --
Martyred and/or imprisoned
For a righteous cause

And some leaders
Neither have pulpit nor podium to teach us.
It's there circumstance that leads us
In to the cruel consciousness
That we must wage on
In our struggle for justice --
In an anal system
Where a gavel strikes malicious intent --
Wrongly convicting the innocent to life
And letting murderers escape sentence.

The Blackman remains a target
As his freedom lays on the balance --
Of fake ass civil right leaders
Too complacent to take the challenge --
To fight for their life, our integrity,
For righteousness to have a second chance.

I lose hope in a future
For the Blackman's unified mental freedom.
For only then shall ye god be worthy
Of the Most High's kingdom.

And the struggle, is the struggle,

Still the struggle nothing differs.
I lay shame wishing the finger
Behind the trigger,
Would have answered that call for this --
Quote unquote "Conscious Nigga"

For my wish was to die for what I believed in
Yet knowing the truth covered by lies
I form a rebellion
And fall deeper and deeper in sin
Looking for that spiritual awakening --
That can please me like that yesterday love
Because a woman
Will always judge another man
By that bad man
That dealt her a miserable hand
But can never see the good in men
Like that good man she let go.

And likewise --
Although much of what I was taught
Be the truth I know.
I still form conflicts of doubt
And uncertainty in my mind
As priest and pastors
Continue to enter temples from behind
There wicked predilections
Escaping justice each and every time.

But the saint's sin is sovereign
Under the lordship of Christ
So they deceive and entice the innocent
Never paying the price.

And although I may forgive them in my heart,
I could never forgive myself --
Not even in part.
For I feel like a soldier with no worth --
One who has lost her crown --
Wishing I'd died laying there on that ground,
With loaded AK at my head and feet,
Instead of riddled with fear as I speak --
Depleting my divinity and maiming my potential.

And I stand here eyes shut as I lose my mental
I pray to the only one I know is true
And Most High I know that you know it's you.
It's you who has the Glory
And you who has the Praise.
And if I may take a humbling moment of your time
For this question I must raise
Will you please protect my children
From devilish ways?

For I had not the tenacity
To resist that being,
That carries the devil's characters
In my genes --
Of laziness, procrastination,
And low self-esteem.
And I thank you for giving me
The eyes for seeing.

Although I block much of your light --
This wounded souljah still has just a little fight

And although I may never be a leader
I will never ever again

Become a follower of a follower
Because even Satan
Bowed before the Most High's throne
So I worship The Most High, Al Aliyu --
Him alone.

And fools go
Where angels fear to tread --
For they choose to worship
A follower instead.

So he who has an ear let him understand!
With the power of the Most High in your hand --
And his divinity in your blood,
Arise to the occasion!
Be that vehicle of information
To strike down fear, ignorance,
Mythology and mis-education --
And pave the way
For the next generation!
For it is written --
Ye are god -- and shall inherit all nations.
Ase.

Lamentations of the Beast's Prey

Dragged into the streets like a dog
We lie choking in our own blood.
Murdered for no other purpose
than the hate that runs through their veins.
The color of our skin makes us a prisoner
in this cultural diaspora we call home

And I cry --
cry because I can't help from wondering why --
why is it all worth it?
Why struggle to be here
in a struggle that never ends?

I wish I could close a blind eye
and see lilies and daffodil delusions of equality
But the bitterness of reality
shows me Trayvon Martin, Jordan Davis, Anna Brown
and so many others.

The other day
an African called my brother a Nigga
And my heart broke as --
as if they were speaking to me.
Because I'm an orphan in this home
where my false family treats me like shit --
And my own kin disowns me.

In my soul, I am just as black as he --
blacker than the mass that embraces the universe --
Blacker than the waters of Nun --
where God walked upon the face of the deep,
before he created the light,

132

that gave birth to the beginning of chaos,
bloodshed and hate --
Black as peace and balance --
black as he.
But in his eyes I am a Nigga too.
And I cry --
cry because I can't help from wondering why --
why is it all worth it?

What will it take to make him see
inside of me, my soul is free?
I don't care how many shackles he places on me,
I am mentally free --
Although physically I bleed.

The slave would rather die and take his child's life,
than to have him suffer enslavement.
And if you really believed
that God has a better place than you would too.
Because you see --
whether heaven exist or not --
whether we just fade into the black --
I'd rather be dead than to feel this pain.

The pain that reminds me
we will never raise from this state.
I've watched many martyrs die
struggling towards that sense of equality
and utopian fantasy --
Just to see we've settled for crumbs
from the Beast's plate.

And it's easy --
I know, to give up the battle

and just find a complacent place.
It eases the pain –
believe me this burnt out soldier knows.

And sometimes I wish God would take me out
of my conscious mind,
And allow me to vacation in that blissful land
of ignorance and shameless ignominy.
Then I wouldn't cry --
cry because I still wonder why --
why waste our time,
Trying to wake the dead.
This horse has been beaten
over 400 feet into the ground --
But we still try to ride it high.

And so I stand bare in the battlefield,
hoping, waiting for the beast to strike
Hoping that God has mercy
and relieves me of this pain.
Because you see --
I am never in fear of the beast killing me.
No, no.
Because in that final breath that i take,
it is he that shall die.
He would have just murdered his hate,
bigotry, jealousy and greed.
And it is I that has been freed from him.

I who no longer cry.
I no longer wonder why.
As I fade into the black,
I am finally free from this pain --
Free from undue blame, plots and exploitations,

false indoctrinations and inferior incantations --
Free from his feast of prejudice and
malicious manipulation --
Free from disrespect, forsaken fortitude,
lost integrity, and self-contempt.

But until then --
as another soul falls by the hand of injustice
As we continue to turn a complacent cheek --
Sell our own to the highest bidder
Snort the silver cloud made of smoke and mirrors
I continue to watch my people
Fall deeper and deeper to the wayside

And I cry --
Cry because I have no answers
As to what will it take and why --
Why is it all worth the struggle?

Indelible Stain

I want to leave a print upon the world
Like turkey and stuffing traditions,
Creeping their way into conscious cultures,
Melting away truths in every morsel,
As you join illegal settlers' complaints
Against indigenous illegal immigrants.

I want to leave stains upon the world
Like trends and stereotypes, and hypnotic indoctrinations,
That tears down walls of integrity and fortitude like Jericho.
Only I want to build them up
With a titanium metal unknown to this realm,
So when people see it, like the pyramids of Egypt,
It remains for thousands of years,
And motherfuckers still don't know how I built it.

I want to leave imprints upon your brain,
That will seep into your DNA,
And like a virus infect you with consciousness --
And destroy any progenitor ignorance,
That can, will or has surfaced in your mind and heart --
So that you can see how detrimental it is
To tear down the walls in your own home,
To use as a foundation for another --
Leaving your children exposed to unnatural disasters,
Chemical, genetic, trendy and techno warfare.

I want to leave indentations upon nations,
So that you can see your vitiligo of the brain
Is no longer and illness or disease,
But a self-induced Uncle Ruckus temporary fix,
You hope can erase the indelible pain --

Not realizing the only cure
Stands back at that crossroad of emancipation
From physical slavery into a mental fetter --
Because the only way you are going to be treated
Like you're not a slave -- is if you stop thinking like one.

I want to leave doors open to your psyche,
So that charismatic Nobel peace speakers
Can be exposed in autumn and stand bare as trees --
Especially those infested with ticks and bugs.
And the only way for the rest of us trees in the orchard are to
survive,
Is if his infectious layer of lies are stripped away,
And the only thing that he and the rest of the world can see,
Is that window seat to bare truth.
And he stands to represent someone that has the fortitude
To be cut down for honor and integrity,
Rather than a soul leaving rings and impressions
Of lies and cowardliness in his- story (history).

I want to leave a hotline to your heart,
So that populations can overcome that abused wife syndrome --
And realize how much you can do better without him --
And open your eyes to see the different between justice being
served,
And a conspiracy to rob you of your resource.
And that every noble murder is not justified,
When in the shadows of equality, a Controlling Intelligent Army,
Is creeping about upon its belling,
Injecting its venom into plights and public --
Blinding them so that they can't see
That a demand for change of regime in a third world country,
Is no different than taking over the street of a corporation,
In efforts to save the economic future of our nation.

137

I want to leave a tight beat to a perfect lyric,
So that you can see the harm
In stripping away a bass line and live percussions --
And replacing it with a falsetto or false echo
Of R&B and synthesized vibrations --
Seeping in your soul like a hypnotic mantra --
Stealing the light and strength that kept you strong
Through lashings whips that stripped pride, integrity and
self-love.
And the only way a kingdom can ever come from above,
Is if you free your mind and reunite yourself
With the beats and tones of Al Kuwn (the universe).
Now they called you Coon
But didn't know they were calling you
9 ether creative forces of the universe.

I want to leave ending with true beginnings,
And holistic healing concepts and realities
That everything we ever needed was put here
Before religious crusades, peacemaking killing squads,
And avaricious powers,
So that you will overstand --
That if we truly gave power to the beast --
I said, if we truly *gave* power to the beast --
Then we are the gods that can take his head,
And free land and country from that iron machine
That consumes this nation,
Before it becomes as desolate as our souls.

I want to leave a creative consciousness,
So that you can fashion concepts
That separating you from your culture
Is like separating you from your soul,

For the sole purpose of stealing your god given inheritance --
That divinity in your bloodline, intertwined with your ancestors --
Your celestial fathers.
You are the masters of your own destiny.
Yet it is for you to take hold.
Command the universe and it will bow to you
As the mysteries once told.
Find that light in the darkness
And become that lighthouse
That paves the way for a new birth of conscious beings.
For ye are gods --
And all of ye are the children of the Most High.

I want to leave an indelible stain,
That brings about a plethora of change,
So that the only thing that remains
Throughout generations and time,
Is a universal language of harmony, peace, and love.
Ase!

Talisman for Shimon and James

If I had anything to tell you --
words to leave you --
I leave you with an apology...
Apologizing for being so weak that I had not
The fortitude to raise you to be strong.
I had not the tenacity to build myself up,
So that you will continue to climb heights
That I could not even fathom.
For this I apologize --
For beating my fears into you,
My illness into you.
So afraid to be bold and me,
Talking about freedom and
Living like a slave.

If I have anything to tell you,
I'd tell you to be free.
Not just free of mind,
But free in spirit and body.
Free of the fear of what life can bring.
And if you allow it, it will bring you
Disappointments and let downs.
But in that case you don't have
Anyone to blame but yourself.

Because as long as you can breathe evenly,
And as long as you are vertical,
As long as you know red is red, and white is white,
And green is green, and greed is greed,
And envy is envy, and hatred is hatred,
And oppression is oppression,
And ignorance is ignorance,

And shame is shame,
And laziness is failure,
And procrastination is regression,
And kindred is community,
And community is unity,
And unity is consciousness,
And consciousness is culture,
And culture is freedom,
And freedom is of the mind,
Body and spirit --
And spirit is of the soul
That links you to your over-soul
Nature, the universes, galaxies,
And dimensions.

As long as you know these things,
Then you should be able to become anything,
Or hold any positive position in existence.
As long as you aspire to be
The solution to the Nubian's problem...
Because point blank,
if you are not part of the solution,
then you are part of the problem
There is no wading in the between.
And the black devil is the most
Detrimental to his race.
So respect them even if they
Don't respect themselves.

So if I leave you anything, I leave you
With these words so that you know
Where you came from...
Not from the abused bodies riddled by drugs,
Or consumed by alcohol,

Or a chemically challenged brain,
From genetic infirmities.
I speak to you from
Before the ships came ashore,
Before your kingdom and soil
Was torn asunder.
I speak to you from the beginning.

You are 9 ether creative forces
Of the universe
Father of civilization
Kings from Queens
And Queens from Kings
Elevated to deities
And Gods and Goddesses
Eneads and Ogdads
Kachina, Umarway,
Shushukiy, Ginwin
Ra, Osiris, Aset, Horus
Orisha, Ogun, Oşun, Şango
Obatallah, Yemaja, Eloheem.
Ye are gods and all of Ye
Are the children of the Most High,
But like men you will die.

So as long as you know these things
then you have no excuse,
From becoming whatever positive role
The universe allows for you.
You are the masters
Of your own destiny,
And it is your responsibility
To bring into this age of
Shadowed consciousness

And blazing ignominy
A generation of Nubians
New beings of conscious autonomy,
To invoke physical, liberty
That will decant into
The next generation.

Now that is real truism
Like a motherfucker.

So if I can leave you anything,
I leave you with the awareness --
That anything you need to know
Is at your feet.
For that seventh seal was broken
And all the knowledge in the universe
Is at your disposal.
All the stones have been unturned
So there is no excuse for you not to succeed

You are May 8th survivors
With guns at your face against your spines
You have the bones
Of those whose backs were
Broken, scarred and tarred
Raped, lynched, beaten
Bludgeoned and burned
And still manage, to sing,
To find love, forgiveness --
Hell, to crack a smile
And try to fit in.
But it's not your place
To fit in.
It is your place to resurrect your

Own empires.
So get ye from under his umbrella,
For I have said therein there is no reign for
Your head.

If I leave you with anything
Teach your children
In order to form kingdoms
They must lay mental bricks...
brick by brick,
Building conscious towers of,
not musical babble,
but of harmony
that will open doorways to EL (Babel).

To be leaders and proprietor they
Must be undertakers.

This is my stone,
Indelibly carved in ink upon paper.
Let it be your shield of protection
Let it be your Psalms 109,
Your Ikhlas, Falaq, Kafiruwn, Nas.
Let it seep into your chest so that
You will not forget
Because Adam (Zakar) failed to
Warn Eve (Nakaybah) about the nature
Of the beast.
So it's important that I don't
Make that same mistake with you.
Because smoke and mirrors
Can make political bullshit
Justifiable and sweet

144

And the shit you consume
Will eventually fuck with your mind

Know who you are
Where you come from
And know your truths.
Seek knowledge from the
Cradle to the grave
It is your two edge sword
Your armor,
The fiber that binds
The body to the soul
The conduit to spirituality
This is my scepter to you
So guard your rights
And never let them steal
Your crown.

If I leave you anything
I leave you these words
Like talismans
To protect you
Revelations pour out from me like
The melting of flesh
Dripping into ball point vials
That bleeds me onto pages

Each leaf is my flesh
This book my body
These words my soul
I am thy Eucharist,
Imbibe me like an elixir

And vomit up his disease of
Inferiority, ignominy, ignorance
Low self-esteem, self-hate
Because I've spent my life trying to teach you better
So consume the jewel of me
And nourish yourself with my consciousness,
My integrity, culture, self-love,
Build from it determination, fortitude and veracity
Speak to your children my words
And resurrect the better part of me

Know this
This life will have happiness
It will have pain
You must be strong enough
To endure, strong enough
To stand for something
And strong enough to
Live and die for what
You believe in
Therein lies the completion of life.

If I leave you anything
I leave you this book
This book is the purest
Form of love I could
Give you
I leave you this book
I leave you me
For all your eternity.

Excerpt from the novel Ambiquity. An Erotic Mystery by Diane Vincent

CHAPTER 1

*F*rail from dehydration, her blood pumping what little her anemic body had to the aching muscles in her stomach from its disgorging of amitriptyline and paroxetine, Rachel tried to block out the rape three weeks prior that led to her failed suicide by focusing on the harbor in the distance. She forced chapters to open in her mind of vestiges when Pastor Alfred and Sister Victoria would take Rachel and her siblings on ferry rides in their attempt to behave like a real family. She recalled how Pastor Alfred's eyes would light up when he spoke about the geological history of the Hudson River and how the estuaries formed by the flooding of river-eroded or glacially-scoured valleys during the Holocene epoch when the sea level began to rise. Once productive and fertile it now suffers from sewage and chemical contamination. Pastor Alfred would go on speaking about the pollution in the Hudson, giving explicit and repulsive details about the waste and drug needles in the river while Rachel, Junior, Tadasha, Taddy for short, and Virginia tried to scuff down funnel cakes without being grossed out by the topic.

Rachel was ordered by the court to undergo psychiatric treatment after the doctors at Bellevue suggested she might be bipolar and/or borderline schizophrenic. The court referred her to Seabrook House, a private substance abuse rehabilitation center where Rachel could receive treatment for her drug addiction and mental health, while avoiding negative publicity. She was assigned therapy with Dr. Nadiya Hunt, who also worked with the Woman's Health Project. It was during one of her visits to the center that Rachel discovered she was pregnant as a result of her rape.

"You know Rachel we've been meeting for three weeks and I think it's time we discuss why we are here."

"I don't know about you but I'm here because the court ordered me to be here. I thought you knew that."

"I'm not talking about what forced you to come here. I'm referring to the reason you were forced to come and what cause the problem."

With her attention broken from the wasteland of images in her past Rachel turned to stare at Dr. Hunt. She hated being forced to bring up arduous thoughts she intensely tried to forget, but indulged it, not only because she was charged to, but because she also enjoyed the lewd mental jaunts she'd occasionally take of her and Dr. Hunt, admiring her beautiful tropical cocoa complexion, full erect lips and deep set lavishing eyes, with an innate allure that kept Rachel's laced boy shorts moist. She could get lost in the journey up her long toned legs for days. Although Dr. Hunt dressed very modest in clothing she purposely picked to cloak her Amazon physique, Rachel knew she was built like a goddess. She longed to brush the string of natural mahogany pressed hair away that caressed Dr. Hunt's high cheek bone and delicate jaw line, her ends just grazing the breast that made Rachel salivated. She smiled relishing the occasional triumph she felt as her flirtatious gazes created an uneasiness that caused Dr. Hunt to stir in her chair. Clearing her throat Dr. Hunt would pretend she was not affected by the wanton stares by avoiding eye contact directing her attention to her notes as she spoke to Rachel. Snickering to inform Dr. Hunt she was not feigned in the least, Rachel removed her gaze and focused on the classical collection Dr. Hunt had on her shelf.

"Georgi Tutev. I love this. Rachel said as she picked up the album to smell the vinyl. "May I." Dr. Hunt gestured for her to go ahead. Rachel smiled as if someone just gave her the go ahead to unwrap her Christmas gift early. She carefully removed the record from the folder and placed it on the antique turntable. "You know the needle on these things are very heavy and can mess up a cherished record like this one. You really should look into getting a lighter turntable. Rachel placed the record on the turntable and powered on the record player watching the needle as it glided to the record. As she stood erect, Dr Hunt watched her patiently, admiring her six feet, one inch stature illuminated by the five o'clock sun above the metropolis. Rachel was beautifully proportioned from head to toe. Her long graceful neck was always poised to perfection. Her black and burnt sienna hair was cut in a retro feathered hairstyle that was incandescent against the sun's rays as if it were aflame. She had the kind of attractiveness that was strikingly beautiful. And she wore it with an 'I'll be damned' kind of cockiness that made her even more enthralling in spite of the four inch scar on her cheek she received as a result of her attack. Rachel smiled, swaying momentarily, taking in the eccentric and classical style of Tutev.

"That's a dramatic piece," Dr. Hunt commented.

"His music defines my life. Sometimes I feel like I'm walking and moving in a Metamorphis or Calvinomuosaik theme. You know what I mean."

"Well I know what it's like to feel confused and misunderstood at the same time."

"Exactly."

"So are you going to answer the question?"

"Question? Oh yes, why are we here? Well I'm assuming you are here because you have a medical degree, which separates you from the psychologist and gives you the authority to zap me if need be. And... well... I guess I'm here because I've gain sort of an ill contempt for this addiction we call life. Funny when you think of it, seeing it's probably the only addiction I'm willing to kick

149

without therapy and the only one I'm receiving therapy for to keep up. Ironic don't you think?"

"So that's how you view life, as an addiction."

"Isn't it? I mean, it deals us such a shitty hand. Sometimes we'll do anything to hold on to it. Take anything and do anything to keep it going, knowing that if we let it go there is a better place, or so we're told. Doesn't that sound like a drug? Isn't that what you doctors tell a junky? If you stop taking drugs you'll have a better life."

"I never looked at life that way. I've always viewed it as a journey in a dimension to learn what we need in order to elevate to a higher existence. If we fail that lesson we possibly repeat it or we don't elevate. Either that or we just exist as energy in one life form governing our own energy flow of existence until we change energy forms."

"Well that's no fun. But then again, if you look at it that way, then it might curve a lot of desire for success and wealth. We are all basically the same infinitesimal elements of existence – no one greater than the next. That can be comforting for a fuck up like me and the fucked up life I'd been dealt."

"You ready to talk about it?"

"No, but I supposed that's the purpose of me being here, to discuss my past so that I can come to terms with why I am so fucked up, in order to get better. And we do want me to get better, right?"

"Yes I do. But do you want to get better Rachel?" Rachel looked down evading eye contact by playing nervously with the buttons on her silk blouse.

"I suppose so. I just wish sometimes I can take a vacation from myself, you know." Rachel raised her head and looked desperately into Dr. Hunts eyes. "Wish I can just take leave of my past, my thoughts and just cease everything. Be blank just for a moment."

"A lot of people say meditation can give you a moment of the solitude you seek."

"I tried that. Can't get my mind to shut the fuck up. Can't get it to stop rewinding the images."

"What images."

"Me at seven mostly and a little before. When hell started I guess. Mostly then because I keep thinking, what if it never happened? What if I never got adopted? What if my mother never killed herself in that hotel, would I be this way?"

"What happened at seven Rachel?"

CHAPTER 2

Hayward St. Yonkers, NY May 1990

Gospel music was often played in the basic colonial style Yonkers home, just enough to notice it in the background, underscoring the pictures of Jesus and his disciples' Last Super, the apocalyptic angels, President John F Kennedy and Dr. Martin Luther King Jr. An upright mahogany piano supported an altar with a ghastly crucifix of an anorexic depiction of Jesus suffering on the cross, a white and red candle with a golden kylix in the center of a silver serving tray and an alabaster box filled with myrrh and gold coins. Young Alfred Henry Pendergrass II, or simply Junior, frowned up his Vaseline shinned, chocolate, plump face as his older sister Virginia tightened his tie around his neck. Her Shirley Temple curls bobbed up and down every time Alfred tried to jerk himself free of her grasp.

"Junior will you stand still so I can finish tightening your tie? You're gonna make us late for church."

"It's too tight. I feel like you're tryna lynch me."

"Oh Junior stop being so dramatic and let your sister straighten out your tie. Don't know why you want to walk around lookin' so triflin' all the time. And Tadasha tell Rachel to hurry out of that bathroom and come downstairs before she makes us late. Tadasha shot to attention like a marine, obeying her mother with a "yes Ma'am" and trotted up the stairs with her huge yellow bow dancing up and down, side to side, on her plump bottom.

Rachel stood in the mirror looking at the dress that used to be Virginia's wondering why her mother insisted on giving her hand-me-downs from someone who was at least three inches shorter and two sizes bigger than she. The dress always looked frumpy and awkward on her. And her mother's infatuation with dresses that looked like they came out of a Baby Jane movie made it look even worse.

"I hate this stupid bow. I feel just like some farm girl that just got dropped out of the sky in a place where she don't belong."

"Well you need to find Todo and come on downstairs. Mama said hurry up before you make us late for church. And you know if you make us one minute late you're gonna feel it for ten minutes later. And ten minutes of that switch seems like a lifetime girl, so come on."

"I ain't scared of no switch. It ain't new to me. Seems like she beats me just for the sun comin' up."

"She beats you because of that fast mouth of yours. Now hurry up Rachel before you get us both in trouble. And unlike you I'm too pretty to be all whelped up."

151

"You too fat to even feel the hit anyway. All that fat cushioning the blow."

"I'ma tell Mama you talkin' about me with your ugly stick self, look like a daddy long legs."

"I'ma get you." Rachel chased after Tadasha and the two girls trampled downstairs with shrilling laughter that caught everyone's attention.

"Stop all that foolishness before I get a switch to you. Come on in here and get your coats on before you make us late for service. Running around here like you ain't got the sense God gave you. I swear Rachel, I don't care how much I try to train you, you still got that wildness of your mama in you. Done messed up your dress, got it all frumpy lookin'."

"It was already that way, 'cause it don't fit right."

"That's because you're tall as a giraffe, only seven years old and already three inches taller than Virginia and she's eleven."

"Well that's why people think you're my real mama, because you're tall too. You're taller than Pastor Alfred."

"I'm the only mama you ever really had, and don't you forget that. Now come put this coat on and stop with that smart lip before it gets a cause to be fattened. That's what you want?"

"No Ma'am."

"Virginia, get my hat off the table in the living room and bring it out to me. Pastor Alfred, are you ready?"

"Yes Sister Victoria. I'm right here at the door with Al Junior," Pastor Alfred said in his usual low trembling voice. Rachel wondered why Pastor Alfred always spoke like one of those witnesses on a crime show that was about to testify in a trial against a murderer. He spoke nervous and never any higher than two octaves above a whisper no matter how mad he was, which seemed like he felt he wasn't entitled to get often. He usually let Sister Victoria get her way most of the time. Rachel resolved he probably was scared of Sister Victoria since she towered over his small five-seven frame. He reminded her of the picture of Jack Sprat in the nursery rhyme. If Rachel wasn't constantly reminded that her mother was a junky that committed suicide and left her baby for dead she would be convinced Sister Victoria and Pastor Alfred were her real parents, because she figured she would have gotten her height from Sister Victoria and her skinniness from Pastor Alfred. Then again Sister Victoria being her mama wouldn't make much sense anyway. She knew her mother's name was Saccharin Walters. Everyone called her Sassy for short. She married her father Victor Sharp straight out of college, and then started a store corner church in Harlem that was somewhat successful. They said her father was known for his shoes. All Rachel would hear was, "I remember your father and those Gators he used to wear. He was a sharp brother." That was it. No one knew what happened to him after her mother killed herself. It was like he dropped off the face of the earth. All Rachel knew was that he didn't stick

152

around for whatever reason to raise her, so she had two choices, settle for the fact that her parents didn't love her enough to stick around and raise her, or convince herself that her father was a good man and was chased off by Sister Victoria and Pastor Alfred, who thought they could do a better job raising her. She chose the latter because it was easier on her emotions.

Rachel watched Sister Victoria as she mounted the yellow silk hat with huge white roses around it upon her head, making her mother look even taller, almost too tall to go out the door without slumping down a little to avoid hitting the top of the door frame.

"CRASH!!!" Rachel's journey into her onerous pass was interrupted by a loud crashing outside of Dr. Hunt's office. A sequence of clangorous sounds followed with several orderlies' voices shouting, "Grab her arm." And a women saying, "Please don't hurt my baby."

"Excuse me Rachel," Dr. Hunt said, as she rose from her chair to see what the commotion was about. She closed the door behind her, but Rachel followed her and cracked it open to see what was going on. A very huge teenage girl was futilely being subdued by seven orderlies after her mother admitted her into the rehab center.

"Please forgive me baby, but I can't see you hurt yourself any longer. Mommy loves you." A hefty woman shouted at her daughter. "Baby don't fight them. It's for your own good."

"No!" The huge girl shouted. I don't want to be in here. I'll quit on my own!" The girl flipped one of the orderlies over her shoulder like a pillow.

"What is going on here," Dr. Hunt shouted. Suddenly everyone froze for about two second as if Dr. Hunt waved a magical wand or pressed a time watch that stopped the entire world at her will.

"I don't want to be in this place! You can't make me stay here!" The girl shouted. Dr. Hunt looked at the orderlies and nurses scornfully.

"You all know the procedure with combative patients. Why wasn't it carried out?"

Is she kidding, the orderly on the floor said, holding his bruised arm from the crash to the floor. "We tried. She won't let us give her a sedative. We were barely able to get her into the center after she found out why she was here. She is on PCP and..."

"Shut up." The huge girl said prying her hands away from another orderly and slapping the one that spoke so hard his head turned ninety degrees. The burning and pain from the slap felt as if he'd been hit with a hot frying pan. The nurses and orderlies continue to struggle. One of the doctors called the police that patrolled the center outside and they were now present. One of the officers put his hand on his weapon, while the other pulled out his stun gun.

"No! Uh, uh," Dr. Hunt shouted. Suddenly Rachel came out the office laughing very hard. Everyone stopped and looked at her including the huge girl.

"Oh my God," Rachel continued to laugh. "Did you see the way she slapped the shit out of him. Yo she punked you hard son." Rachel laughed so hard, she provoked the girl to laugh. Rachel reached out for the girl to tap her hand and the girl did in response. "What's your name," Rachel asked.

"Sha'Darien." The girl responded. Rachel continued to hold Sha'Darien's right hand and then rubbed her arm as she circled her, moving the orderlies out of her way that were holding Sha'Darien. She let her hand trace across Sha'Darien's back sending chills throughout the girl's body. Sha'Darien could not take her eyes off the stunning woman that seemed to captivate everyone.

"How old are you Sha'Darien," Rachel asked looking seductively into the girl's eyes.

"Nineteen," Sha'Darien responded, her eyes frozen on Rachel.

"Nineteen, huh." Good 'cause I like them thick bone and roughish." Rachel took her hand and stroked Sha'Darien's left arm before taking hold of her left hand. She could feel Sha'Darien flutter from her touch and laughed to herself, proud she still had what it took to make a woman beckon to her touch. She took her middle finger and stroked the inside of Sha'Darien's palm lightly before releasing it. Sha'Darien inhaled deeply, her huge bosoms rising and settling as everyone watching instinctively followed. Rachel walked away and everyone watched her as if she were on a runway modeling an infamous designer's outfit. "I'll see you later Dr. Hunt. Thanks for the session." Sha'Darien stared at Rachel until she disappeared around a corner, and then looked at her mother.

"How long do I have to be in here," She asked. Everyone's shoulders relaxed with Sha'Darien's mother, who smiled warmly at her daughter.

"Until you are well. But I will come see you every day... or... or when they have visiting days. But I'll call every day to check up on you, I promise. I love you baby, and I just want you to get some help before you really hurt yourself this time." Sha'Darien looked at her mother, then at the nurses, orderlies and police disdainfully, and then back at her mother and nodded her head.

"They are not going to hurt me are they," Sha'Darien asked Dr. Hunt.

"No Sha'Darien, not at all. We just want to help you get better and be the best you can be.

"Will I have therapy sessions with you too?"

"I can request that if you like." Sha'Darien nodded. Dr. Hunt put her arms around Sha'Darien and guided her to triage, where they could examine her before they admitted her. "We just need to take some blood and check some vital signs to see how much drugs are in your system and how it might be affecting you. Okay?

"Yes Ma'am. You think they can help me lose some weight too... not too much though... I like being thick, just not fat." Dr. Hunt laughed.

"I'm sure we can suggest some healthy diets and exercise regiments that can help you lose a few pounds if you like," Dr. Hunt said squeezing Sha'Darien affectionately, before directing her into the triage room, where a nurse practitioner waited to take Sha'Darien's vital signs. Dr. Hunt took Sha'Darien's chart from the practitioner and looked over it briefly noticing Sha'Darien's last name, Rossie. "Take good care of Ms. Rossie. She is a very special patient of mine." Sha'Darien smiled at Dr. Hunt and humbly sat down on the patient's bed. Dr. Hunt rubbed her arm affectionately before leaving the room. Sha'Darien looked at the practitioner fearfully.

"Okay I'm afraid of needles, so please don't hurt me."

Dr. Hunt walked into her office and noticed someone had lain a manila folder on her desk with the name Sha'Darien Rossie attached to the tab. She sat down at her desk and opened up the file to review it. Her mind could not stop replaying the way Rachel took control of the incident that had just occurred with Sha'Darien. *How could she have known Sha'Darien would respond to her that way? I guess she figured she was just a big girl that needed love.* Dr. Hunt recalled the sensual way Rachel's hands danced across Sha'Darien's back and the way Sha'Darien's body trembled slightly in response. Dr. Hunt smiled and bit her lip admiring the slick way Rachel seductively flirted with the huge girl, sliding her finger in the palm of her hand. She noticed it because she remembered her best friend in college doing the same thing to her once, and how it sent sensations throughout her body before connecting to her root chakra. It amazed her still how there are so many erogenous zones on the body. Her pondering was interrupted by the director of the facility, Dr. Debra Watson, knocking on her door then entering the office.

"Hey Naddie, I heard the police had to be called in on a patient being admitted, because no one could subdue her, then miraculously Ms. Pendergrass comes along and calms the woman down with one touch like she was the second coming. What the heck happened? Dr. Hunt looked at Dr. Watson and shook her head as she began to laugh.

Made in the USA
Charleston, SC
20 June 2014